CARE OF THE SOUL

CARE OF THE
SOUL

HOW TO ADD DEPTH AND
MEANING TO YOUR EVERYDAY LIFE

THOMAS MOORE

HarperCollins*Publishers*

CARE OF THE SOUL. Copyright © 1998 by Thomas Moore. All rights reserved. Printed in the United States of America. No part of this book may be used or reproduced in any manner whatsoever without written permission except in the case of brief quotations embodied in critical articles and reviews. For information address HarperCollins Publishers, Inc., 10 East 53rd Street. New York, NY 10022.

HarperCollins books may be purchased for educational, business, or sales promotional use. For information please write: Special Markets Department, HarperCollins Publishers, Inc., 10 East 53rd Street, New York, NY 10022.

FIRST EDITION

Produced by The Book Laboratory, Inc.
Designed by Bullet Liongson

Library of Congress Cataloging-in-Publication Data

Moore, Thomas, 1940–
   Illustrated care of the soul / Thomas Moore. — 1st ed.
    p. cm.
   Rev. ed. of: Care of the soul. c1992.
   Includes bibliographical references.
   ISBN 0-06-757511-0
    1. Spiritual life. 2. Psychology, Religious. 1. Moore, Thomas,
1940– Care of the soul. 11. Title.
   BL624.M663 1998   98-23018
   158. 1—dc21

98 99 00 01 02 ❖ 10 9 8 7 6 5 4 3 2 1

Contents

Introduction

THE MIND WORKS WITH IDEAS, THE BODY WITH MUSCLES, AND THE SOUL WITH images. It is entirely appropriate that *Care of the Soul* be presented with images that convey some of the mystery of the soul's many facets. Prose comes up short as it attempts to describe what it is like to live from the soul. But images take us to a deeper place where the soul has its home, and so they show us more faithfully what the soul is and how it goes about giving us our humanity and ordinary life its beauty.

People often ask: How can I learn more about the soul? How can I understand my dreams? How can I find meaning in emotional and physical suffering? I often recommend a thoughtful, contemplative tour of the local art museum or art galleries. A painting is like a mirror—we look into it and see ourselves and our world reflected. All the arts give our lives a mysterious dimension beyond space, time, and literal depth. They bring us into the image world, where meaning and emotions play out.

Not all paintings, musical compositions, and films effectively reveal the soul's nature. Some are limited because the artist is not open to the deeper mysteries but instead merely expresses personal biography or ideology. Self-expression is not as deep-seated as soul-expression. Sometimes art is reactionary, full of agenda, and egotistic. In these cases, the soul stays in hiding. But occasionally a piece of art will be so transparent, so profoundly rooted, and so precisely articulated that the soul shines, and in that meaningful radiance we sense its beauty.

When art reveals the soul, it may have a certain objective quality and may even feel cool because of its deep roots. At other times, captivating art may be so hot with the inspiration of the artist and so alive with his or her presence that individuality is transcended, and soul appears. The soul's radiance sometimes penetrates surface intentions and aesthetic doctrines to waken some hidden spirit in the observer.

I found unexpected pleasure when I first read through this abbreviated text of *Care of the Soul* latticed with a wide variety of images. This, I felt, is the best way to consider the soul—to be stopped on almost every page by an intriguing image that sustains the mystery and at the same time reveals something that words cannot express. The images on these pages, so varied as they evoke a wealth of cultures and artistic visions, show how vast the soul really is and how many ways there are to its mysteries and pleasures.

With the addition of many different images, a mere book becomes a place. Where before we read, now we can stroll. Where before we kept a distance from our subject by means of ideas, now we approach it more intimately and sensuously. Now the body is invited to participate, and soul accordingly shows more of itself. It reveals that it is not abstract but has a certain kind of body, not as sensuous as our physical bodies perhaps, but not as invisible and as intangible as our logic.

I am deeply grateful for the excellent work of Philip Dunn, Malcolm Godwin and Magda Valine. Throughout the process they have been devoted, patient, and receptive. They turned intuitively in the right directions for images that would embody the spirit of *Care of the Soul*. The project began with a remarkable instance of caring for my soul. They criss-crossed England in two cars to rescue me and my family when our travel plans fell apart. On country roads and city streets we discussed the nature of the soul and the kinds of images that would convey its variety and essence. Later, they set to the demanding work of gathering images and placing them in the text, all the while remaining faithful to the long, single, theological, philosophical, and aesthetic discussion we had had above the roar of an engine and the din of traffic.

The soul is to be found in the oddest places. I hope that these images strike readers of *Care of the Soul* and send them off in unexpected directions. I hope the images inspire readers to bring art into their lives intimately and powerfully. I hope a few of these images come to life from the pages and take up residence in the reader's home. My fondest hope is that our culture might learn to live less abstractly and rediscover the central place of images and the arts in our communal lives.

I

CARE OF THE SOUL

John Keats *by Joseph Severn.*

I am certain of nothing
but the holiness of the Heart's affections and the truth of the Imagination.

—John Keats

CHAPTER ONE

Honoring Symptoms as a Voice of the Soul

O NCE A WEEK PEOPLE IN THE THOUSANDS show up for their regular appointment with a therapist. They bring problems they have talked about many times before, problems that cause them intense emotional pain and make their lives miserable. Depending on the kind of therapy employed, the problems will be analyzed, referred back to childhood and parents, or attributed to some key factor such as the failure to express anger, alcohol in the family, or childhood abuse. Whatever the approach, the aim will be health or happiness achieved by the removal of these central problems.

Care of the soul is a fundamentally different way of regarding daily life and the quest for happiness. The emphasis may not be on problems at all. One person might care for the soul by buying or renting a good piece of land, another by selecting an appropriate school or program of study, another by painting his house or his bedroom. Care of the soul is a continuous process that concerns itself not so much with "fixing" a central flaw as with attending to the small details of everyday life, as well as to major decisions and changes.

When Marsilio Ficino wrote his self-help book, *The Book of Life*, five hundred years ago, he placed emphasis on carefully choosing colors, spices, oils, places to walk, countries to visit—all very concrete decisions of everyday life that day by day either support or disturb the soul. We think of the psyche, if we think about it at all, as a cousin to the brain and therefore something essentially internal. But ancient psychologists taught that our own souls are inseparable from the world's soul, and that both are found in all the many things that make up nature and culture.

So, the first point to make about care of the soul is that its goal is not to make life

Above: Mystery *by Odilon Redon, 1905.*
Opposite: Marsilio Ficino, *detail of a painting by Ghirlandaio, 15th century.*

problem-free, but to give ordinary life the depth and value that come with soulful-ness. In a way it is much more of a challenge than psychotherapy because it has to do with cultivating a richly expressive and meaningful life at home and in society.

Getting to Know the Soul

The word *care* implies a way of responding to expressions of the soul that is not heroic and muscular. Care is what a nurse does, and "nurse" happens to be one of the early meanings of the Greek word *therapeia*, or therapy. We'll see that care of the soul is in many ways a return to early notions of what therapy is. *Cura*, the Latin word used originally in "care of the soul," means several things: attention, devotion, husbandry, adorn-ing the body, healing, managing, being anxious for, and worshiping the gods. It might be a good

Non nisi Parvulis.

idea to keep all these meanings in mind as we try to see as concretely as possible how we might make the shift from psychotherapy as we know it today to care of the soul.

This definition of caring for the soul is minimalist. It has to do with modest care and not miraculous cure. But my cautious definition has practical implications for the way we deal with ourselves and with one another. For example, if I see my responsi-bility to myself, to a friend, or to a patient in therapy as observing and respecting what the soul presents, I won't try to take things away in the name of health.

A thirty-year-old woman comes to me for therapy and confesses, "I have a terrible time in relationships because I become too dependent. Help me be less dependent."

I am being asked to take some soul stuff away. I should go to my toolbox and take out a scalpel, extractor, and suction pump. Instead, on the principle of observance, and not inclined in any case to this kind of pilfering, I ask, "What is it you find dif-ficult about dependence?"

"It makes me feel powerless. Besides, it isn't good to be too dependent. I should be my own person."

"How do you know when your dependency is too much?" I reply, still trying to speak for the soul's expression of dependency.

"When I don't feel good about myself."

"I wonder," I continue in the same direction, "if you could find a way to be dependent without feeling disempowered? After all, we all depend on each other every minute of the day."

I notice from the conversation that despite all her enthusiasm for independence, she doesn't seem to enjoy much of it in her life. She is identified with the dependency and sees liberation on the other side. She has also unconsciously bought into the prevailing notion that independence is healthy and that we should correct the soul when it shows some desire for dependence.

Her heroic championing of independence might be a way of avoiding and repressing the strong need of something in her to be dependent.

I had the feeling this woman, as seems often to be the case, was avoiding intimacy and friendship by focusing these qualities into a caricature of excessive dependency. At times we live these caricatures, thinking we are being masochistically dependent, when what we actually are doing is avoiding deep involvement with people, society, and life in general.

Observing what the soul is doing and hearing what it is saying is a way of "going with the symptom." The temptation is to compensate, to be drawn toward the opposite of what is presented. A person fully identified with dependency thinks that health and happiness lie in the achievement of independence. But that move into opposites is deceptive. Oddly, it keeps the person in the same problem, only from the opposite side. The wish for independence maintains the split. A homeopathic move, going with what is presented rather than against it, is to learn how to be dependent in a way that is satisfying and not so extreme as to split dependence off from independence.

Another way of disowning the soul is merely to dip your toes in the sea of fate. A man came to me depressed and completely dissatisfied with his job. He had been working in a manufacturing shop for ten years, and all that time he planned his escape. He was going to go to school and enter a profession that he liked. But while he planned and kept his mind continually on his escape, his work in the shop suffered. Years went by and he was always dissatisfied, hating his job and wishing for the promised land of his ambitions.

"Have you ever thought," I asked him one day, "of being where you are, of entering fully this job that you're putting your time and energy into?"

"It's not worth it," he said. "It's beneath me. A robot could do it better."

"But you do it every day," I observed. "And you do it badly, and you feel bad about yourself for doing it badly."

"You're saying," he said incredulously, "that I should go to this stupid job as if my heart were in it?"

"*You're* in it, aren't you?"

He came back in a week to say that something had changed in him as he began to take his "stupid" job more seriously. It seemed that by entering his fate and emotions he might begin to taste his life and possibly find a way *through* his experience and into his ambitions. The sheep of his work fantasies had been wandering everywhere but in the shop. He had been living an alienated and divided life.

The basic intention in any caring, physical or psychological, is to alleviate suffering. But in relation to the symptom itself, observance means first of all listening and looking carefully at what is being revealed in the suffering. An intent to heal can get in the way of seeing. By doing less, more is accomplished. Observance is homeopathic in its workings rather than allopathic, in the paradoxical way that it befriends a problem rather than making an enemy of it. A Taoist tone colors this care without heroics. The *Tao Te Ching* says (ch. 64), "He brings men back to what they have lost. He helps the ten thousand things find their own nature, but refrains from action." This is a perfect description of one who cares for the soul.

It is not easy to observe closely, to take the time and to make the subtle moves that allow the soul to reveal itself further. You have to rely on every bit of learning, every scrap of sense, and all kinds of reading, in order to bring intelligence and imagination to the work. Yet at the same time, this action-through-nonaction has to be simple, flexible, and receptive. Intelligence and education bring you to the edge, where your mind and its purposes are empty. Many religious rites begin with washing of the hands or a sprinkling of water to symbolize the cleansing of intention and the washing away of thoughts and purposes. In our soul work we could use rites like these, anything that would cleanse our minds of their well-intentioned heroism.

Observance has considerable power. If you observe Christmas, for instance, you will be affected by that special season precisely because of your observance. The mood and spirit of the time will touch your heart, and over time, regular observance may come to affect you deeply. Or if you are a pallbearer at a funeral, if you sprinkle dirt or holy water at the grave, your observance places you deep within the experience of burial and death. You may remember that moment vividly for years. You may dream about it for the rest of your life. Simple gestures, taking place on the surface of life, can be of central importance to the soul.

Modern interventional therapy sometimes tries to solve specific problems and can therefore be carried out on a short-term basis. But care of the soul never ends. The alchemists of the Middle Ages seem to have recognized this fact, since they taught their students that every ending is a beginning. All work on the

Top: Bronze figure of Lao Tzu riding a buffalo, Sung dynasty, 11th century.
Right: Lao Tzu, 18th century, China.

soul takes the form of a circle, a rotation. People in therapy often say to me, "Aren't you tired of hearing the same things over and over again?" "No," I respond. "I'm quite happy with the old stuff." I keep in mind the alchemical circulation. The life of the soul, as the structure of dreams reveals, is a continual going over and over of the material of life.

In memory we never tire of reflecting on the same events. I spent many summers in my childhood on a farm with an uncle who told stories endlessly. This, I now see, was his method of working the raw material of his life, his way of turning his experience round and round in the rotation that stories provide. Out of that incessant storytelling I know he found added depths of meaning. Storytelling is an excellent way of caring for the soul. It helps us see the themes that circle in our lives, the deep themes that tell the myths we live. It would take only a slight shift in emphasis in therapy to focus on the storytelling itself rather than on its interpretation.

Learning to Love the Soul

Freud's *The Interpretation of Dreams* is largely this kind of psychologizing. He analyzes his own dreams and arrives at theory from his self-analysis. He writes as though he is intensely interested in the ways of his own soul. He tells stories and dreams, not unlike my uncle, whose stories also condensed into a theory about life. We could all be a Freud to our own experiences. Taking an interest in the soul is a way of loving it. The ultimate cure, as many ancient and modern psychologies of depth have asserted, comes from love and not from logic. Understanding doesn't take us very far in this work, but love, expressed in patient and careful attention, draws the soul in from its dispersion in problems and fascinations. It has often been noted that most, if not all, problems brought to therapists are issues of love. It makes sense then that the cure is also love.

Taking an interest in one's own soul we begin to see our own complexity. Usually we

Sigmund Freud boards his
first airplane at the age of 70.
Left: Sigmund Freud.

feel that complexity as it hits us unawares from outside, in a multitude of problems and in
confusion. If we knew the soul better, we might be ready for the conflicts of life. I often
have the sense, when someone tells me anxiously about some knot they find themselves
in, that what they perceive as an impossible and painful situation calling for professional
intervention is simply the complexity of human life once again manifesting itself. Most of
us bring to everyday life a somewhat naive psychological attitude in our expectations that

our lives and relationships will be simple. Love of the soul asks for some appreciation for its complexity.

Often care of the soul means not taking sides when there is a conflict at a deep level. It may be necessary to stretch the heart wide enough to embrace contradiction and paradox.

A Taste for the Perverse

One effective "trick" in caring for the soul is to look with special attention and openness at what the individual rejects, and then to speak favorably for that rejected element. We all tend to divide experience into two parts, usually the good and the bad. But there may be all kinds of suspicious things going on in this splitting. We may simply have never considered the value in certain things that we reject. Or by branding certain experiences negative we may be protecting ourselves from some unknown fears.

What I am talking about here is a version of Jung's theory of shadow. For Jung, there are two kinds of shadow: one consists of the possibilities in life that we reject because of certain choices we have made. The person we choose to be, for example, automatically creates a dark double—the person we choose not to be. This compensatory shadow varies from one person to the next. For some people sex and money are looming shadows, while for others they are simply part of life. Moral purity and responsible living can be shadow aspects to some. Jung also believed there is an absolute shadow, not relative to our life choices and habits. In other words, there is evil in the world and in the human heart. If we don't recognize this, we have a naive attitude that can get us into trouble. Jung thought the soul can benefit by coming to terms with both kinds of shadow, losing some of its naive innocence in the process.

As we get to know the soul and fearlessly consider its oddities and the many different ways it shows itself among individuals, we may develop a taste for the perverse. We may come to appreciate its quirks and deviances. Indeed, we may eventually come to realize that individuality is born in the eccentricities and unexpected shadow tendencies of the soul, more so than in normality and conformity. One who cares for the soul becomes someone at ease with idiosyncrasies and the unexpected.

Care of the soul is interested in the not-so-normal, the way that soul makes itself

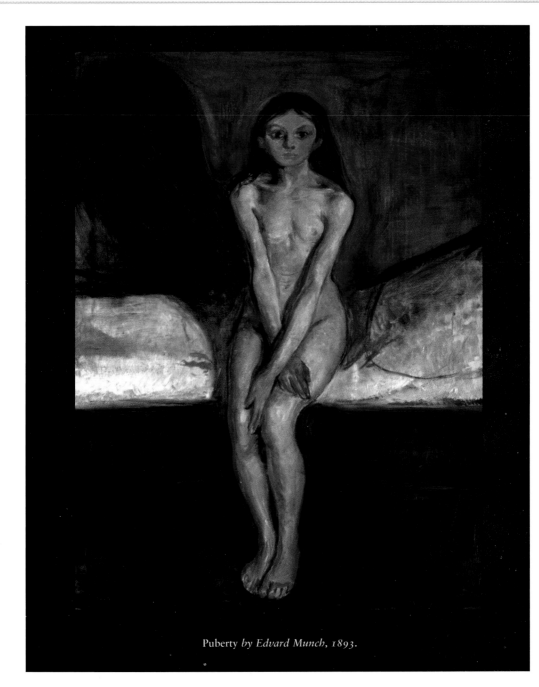

Puberty *by Edvard Munch, 1893.*

Creation *by Hildegard of Bingen.*

felt most clearly in the unusual expressions of a life, even and maybe especially in the problematical ones.

It is no accident that the history of art is filled with grotesque images—bloody and twisted crucifixions, gracefully distorted bodies, and surrealistic landscapes. Sometimes deviation from the usual is a special revelation of truth. When normality explodes or breaks out into craziness or shadow, we might look closely, before running for cover and before attempting to restore familiar order, at the potential meaningfulness of the event. If we are going to be curious about the soul, we may need to explore its deviations, its perverse tendency to contradict expectations. And as a corollary, we might be suspicious of normality. A facade of normality can hide a wealth of deviance, and besides, it is fairly easy to recognize soullessness in the standardizing of experience.

Care Versus Cure

Ancient psychology, rooted in a very different ground from modern therapeutic thinking, held that the fate and character of each of us is born in mystery, that our individuality is so profound and so hidden that it takes more than a lifetime for identity to emerge. Renaissance doctors said that the essence of each person originates as a star in the heavens. How different this is from the modern view that a person is what he makes himself to be.

Care of the soul, looking back with special regard to ancient psychologies for insight and guidance, goes beyond the secular mythology of the self and recovers a sense of the sacredness of each individual life. This sacred quality is not just value—all lives are important. It is the unfathomable mystery that is the very seed and heart of each individual. Shallow therapeutic manipulations aimed at restoring normality or tuning a life according to standards reduces—shrinks—that profound mystery to the pale dimensions of a social common denominator referred to as the adjusted personality. Care of the soul sees another reality altogether. It appreciates the mystery of human suffering and does not offer the illusion of a problem-free life. It sees every fall into

Wheel of Life *by Hildegard of Bingen.*

ignorance and confusion as an opportunity to discover that the beast residing at the center of the labyrinth is also an angel. The uniqueness of a person is made up of the insane and the twisted as much as it is of the rational and normal. To approach this paradoxical point of tension where adjustment and abnormality meet is to move closer to the realization of our mystery-filled, star-born nature.

Obviously, care of the soul requires a different language from that of therapy and academic psychology. Like alchemy, it is an art and therefore can only be expressed in poetic images. Mythology, the fine arts, religions of the world, and dreams provide this priceless imagery by which the soul's mysteries are simultaneously revealed and contained. For guidance we can also turn to many different experts, especially to poetic-minded soul searchers such as the ancient mythographers and tragedians, Renaissance doctors, Romantic poets, and our modern depth psychologists, who

La Minotauromachie *by Pablo Picasso, 1935.*

respect the mystery of human life and who resist the secularization of experience. It takes a broad vision to know that a piece of the sky and a chunk of the earth lie lodged in the heart of every human being, and that if we are going to care for that heart we will have to know the sky and earth as well as human behavior.

The Greeks told the story of the minotaur, the bull-headed flesh-eating man who lived in the center of the labyrinth. He was a threatening beast, and yet his name was Asterion—Star. I often think of this paradox as I sit with someone with tears in her eyes, searching for some way to deal with a death, a divorce, or a depression. It is a beast, this thing that stirs in the core of her being, but it is also the star of her innermost nature. We have to care for this suffering with extreme reverence so that, in our fear and anger at the beast, we do not overlook the star.

II

CARE OF THE SOUL IN EVERYDAY LIFE

Nature and God—I neither knew
Yet Both so well knew me
They startled, like Executors
of My identity.

—Emily Dickinson

CHAPTER TWO

The Myth of Family and Childhood

E TERNITY IS IN LOVE WITH THE PRODUCTIONS OF TIME," says William Blake. The soul prospers in an environment that is concrete, particular, and vernacular. It feeds on the details of life, on its variety, its quirks, and its idiosyncrasies. Therefore, nothing is more suitable for care of the soul than family, because the experience of family includes so much of the particulars of life. In a family you live close to people that otherwise you might not even want to talk to. Over time you get to know them intimately. You learn their most minuscule, most private habits and characteristics. Family life is full of major and minor crises—the ups and downs of health, success and failure in career, marriage, and divorce—and all kinds of characters.

When things go wrong in society, we immediately inquire into the condition of family life. When we see society torn apart by crime, we cry, "If only we could return to the good old days when family was sacred." But were the good old days so good? Was the family ever free of violence? Many people who come to therapy today were raised in the so-called golden age of the family, and yet they tell stories of abuse, neg-

lect, and terrifying moralistic demands and pressures. Looked at coldly, the family of any era is both good and bad, offering both support and threat.

Today professionals are preoccupied with the "dysfunctional family." But to some extent all families are dysfunctional. No family is perfect, and most have serious problems. A family is a microcosm, reflecting the nature of the world, which runs on both virtue and evil.

When I see those three letters "dys-" in "dysfunctional," I think of "Dis," the old Roman name for the mythological underworld. Soul enters life from below, through the cracks, finding an opening into life at the points where smooth functioning breaks down. We bring the Dis-functions of family into the therapy room as problems to be solved or as explanations for current difficulties because intuitively we know that the family is one of the chief abodes of soul. In psychology there is much talk about family, and "family therapy" has become a major form of counseling. By "getting to the root" of present problems in family background, we hope to under-

stand what is going on, and in that understanding we hope to find a cure. But care of the soul doesn't require fixing the family or becoming free of it or interpreting its pathology. We may need simply to recover soul by reflecting deeply on the soul events that have taken place in the crucible of the family.

It is remarkable how often the family is experienced on two levels: the facade of happiness and normality, and the behind-the-scenes reality of craziness and abuse. I have heard many stories over the years of families that are picture-book perfect on the surface—family camping, Sunday dinners, trips, gifts, and play. But beneath it all is the remote father, the hidden alcohol, the abuse of a sister, and midnight violence. Television presents this bifurcation with sitcoms of sweet and successful families followed by news reports of family savagery. Recovery of soul begins when we can take to heart our own family fate and find in it the raw material, the alchemical *prima materia*, for our own soul work.

For this purpose, "family therapy" might take the form of simply telling stories of family life, free of any concern for cause and effect or sociological influence. These stories generate a grand local, personal mythology. The family is to the individual what the origins of human life are to the race.

To care for the soul of the family, it is necessary to shift from causal thinking to an appreciation for story and character, to allow grandparents and uncles to be transformed into figures of myth and to watch certain familiar family stories become canonical through repeated tellings. We are so affected by the scientific tone in education and in the media that without thinking we have become anthropologists and

The Wedding *by Henri Rousseau, 1904-1905.*

sociologists in our own families. Often I will ask a patient about the family, and the answer I get is pure social psychology. "My father drank, and as a child of an alcoholic I am prone to . . ." Instead of stories, one hears analysis. The family has been "etherized upon a table." Even worse is the social worker or psychologist who begins talking about a patient with a singsong list of social influences: "The subject is a male who was raised in a Judeo-Christian family, with a narcissistic mother and a codependent father." The soul of the family evaporates in this kind of reduction.

When we tell stories about the family without judgment and without instant analysis, the literal persons turn into characters in a drama and isolated episodes reveal themselves as themes in a great saga. Family history is transformed into myth.

With this principle in mind, I want to look at family members as imaginal figures and to offer some suggestions for finding the myths in the ordinary roles of family life. For each individual, the myth will be different, and yet certain characteristics are constant. Every family member evokes the archetypal family, the myth in everyday life. The imagination of father, mother and child is vast, and so I can only give some hints toward a way of developing a family imagination, including some references to literature and mythology that offer a path toward understanding the family more imaginally.

The Father

One of the most extraordinary mythic stories from our own collective past, a story as sacred as any in religious literature, is about a man trying to reclaim his fatherhood, a wife longing for her husband, and a son out in search of his lost father. At the beginning of Homer's *Odyssey*, Odysseus is sitting on the seashore in the midst of his unplanned travels following a long, difficult war, wishing to be home with his son, his father, and the mother of his children. In his longing and melancholy he asks a famous question: "Does any person know who his father is?" It's a question many men and women ask in various forms. If my father is dead, or if he was absent and cold, or if he was a tyrant, or if he abused me, or if he was wonderful but is not there for me now, then who is my father now? Where do I get those feelings of protection, authority, confidence, know-how, and wisdom that I need in order to live my life?

Odysseus
and the Sirens.
*Vase painting
from Thebes,
c.430 BCE.*

How can I evoke a fatherly myth in a way that will give my life the governance it needs?

The story of Odysseus gives us many clues toward finding that elusive father. However, it does not begin, as one might expect, with the father in the throes of his adventures, but with the son, Telemachus, distraught at the havoc created in his house by suitors vying for his mother's affections. The story gives us first an image of "absent-father neurosis." Without the father there is chaos, conflict, and sadness. On the other hand, by starting with the unhappiness of Telemachus, the story teaches us that the experience of father includes his absence and the longing for his return. For at the very moment Telemachus is bewailing his situation, Odysseus is on another beach on the same sea, pining for the same conclusion. If we understand *The Odyssey* as one of the stories of the soul's fatherhood, then at that very moment when we feel the confusion of a fatherless life and wonder where he could be, the father has been evoked. As we wonder where he is, he is finding his way back.

During this time of separation, Homer tells us, Odysseus' wife, Penelope, is at home weaving a shroud for Odysseus' father, and every night she unravels what she has woven. This is the great mystery of the soul: whenever something is being accomplished, it is also in some way being undone.

There is something frustrating about the very idea of *The Odyssey*. Why don't the gods look compassionately on this broken family and allow Odysseus to make a beeline home? What possible value is there in this father taking ten years on the sea, telling his stories and surviving his risky adventures, before he can finally return home and restore peace? The only answer I can think of is that this long, dangerous, adventure-filled journey is the making of the father. Odysseus' return to his family is analogous to the Gnostic stories of the soul descending through the planets to earth, picking up along the way the qualities it will need for human life. Who is my father? I won't know until the soul has been on its odyssey and returns with its stories of love, sex, death, risk, and afterlife.

Odysseus goes through many ordeals, so much so that his story looks exactly like an initiation into fatherhood. The centerpiece of his story is a visit to the land of the dead. There he meets recently departed friends, his mother, the blind prophet Tiresias, and other great figures of history. True fatherhood is evoked not by a flexing of muscle but by initiation into family and culture in a profound, transformative way. It may also require a visit to our own depths and a conversing with figures of memory both personal and cultural.

If the father seems absent in families today, that may be because he is absent as a soul figure in the society at large. We have replaced secret wisdom with information. Information does not evoke fatherhood, and it does not effect initiation. Far from visiting the land of the dead, all too often we want to forget the dead and the burden of their lives. Our highly detailed investigations of the murders of the Kennedys and Martin Luther King, Jr., focus on facts and on a solution to the cases, thereby deflecting attention away from the meaning of those assassinations. Yet, *The Odyssey* implies that if we don't visit the land of the dead with reverence and in a spirit of initiation, we will not have a sustaining fatherhood in our collective soul. Without that deep spirit of the father, we are left with father substitutes—people willing to play the part for their own gain, offering superficial tokens of fatherhood, but not the father's soul.

This fatherhood of the soul is a face of what Jung called animus, which can be the father-spirit in a man, woman, family, organization,

Painter of Orythia. Thetis, Zeus and Eos.
Red figure crater from Campania, c. 470-450 BCE.

Odysseus and the Sirens (*detail*), *Volterra, 2nd century* BCE.

nation, or place. A nation might venture out on an odyssey and in the process find a fathering principle that will give it authority and direction. We have to dare to experience the unknown, to open ourselves to unexpected influences on the soul.

The trouble with some of our modern therapies and psychologies is that they aim at goals that are known—fantasies of normality or unquestioned values. One psychologist says that people need to be empowered—that is her definition of health. But there are also times when we may need to be weak and powerless, vulnerable and open to experience, as were Odysseus and Tristan, both of whom used their wits rather than their muscles. Another psychologist says people need to be capable of intimacy—relationship is the ultimate goal. But soul also requires solitude and individuality.

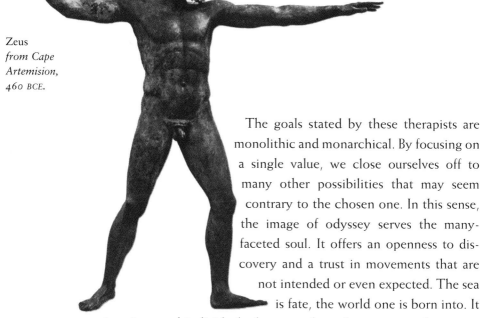

Zeus
*from Cape
Artemision,
460 BCE.*

The goals stated by these therapists are monolithic and monarchical. By focusing on a single value, we close ourselves off to many other possibilities that may seem contrary to the chosen one. In this sense, the image of odyssey serves the many-faceted soul. It offers an openness to discovery and a trust in movements that are not intended or even expected. The sea is fate, the world one is born into. It is unique and individual, always uncharted, teeming with its own dangers, pleasures, and opportunities. One becomes a father to one's own life by becoming intimately acquainted with it and by daring to traverse its waters.

The Odyssey adds an interesting motif to this process. While Odysseus is away from home engaged in his own education for fatherhood, he has a stand-in at home by the name of Mentor, who cares for the house and teaches Telemachus. The father figures in our lives can be of two kinds. They may be substitutes who symptomatically play the role of father for us but interfere with our own fathering odysseys. But some father figures are true mentors, furthering the deep process of fatherhood by understanding their limited role and by not usurping the father's role for themselves, even as they teach and guide. Some teachers don't seem to understand the need in their students to be on an odyssey and to be discovering their own fatherhood. They expect their students to be a copy of themselves and to profess the same values and information. Some business and political leaders see their role in society as promoting their own personal ideologies rather than serving as genuine mentors; they don't understand that the populace must make its own collective odyssey in order to evoke a soulful fatherhood for the society. It takes genuine wisdom to be a mentor, the pleasure of which comes from instilling fatherhood rather than embodying it.

As the Bible gives us an image of a father in the sky, *The Odyssey* tells us about the father who is on the sea. While this second father is "at sea" being fashioned and enlightened, we need mentors, father figures who keep the notion of father alive in us.

Without soulful fathers, our society is left with mere reason and ideology as guides. Then we suffer collective fatherlessness: not having a clear national direction; giving the spoils of a wealthy economy to a few; finding only rare examples of deep morality, law, and community; not seeking out odyssey because we prefer the solid ground of opinion and ideology. To set out on the sea is to risk security, yet that risky path may be the only way to the father.

Culturally we are also suffering from the breakdown of patriarchy. Feminist thought properly criticizes the oppression of women on the part of long-standing male domination, but that political patriarchy is not the patriarchy of the soul. Patriarchy means absolute, profound, archetypal fatherhood. We need a return of patriarchy in this deepest sense, because to vacillate between embracing symptomatic and oppressive fathering on one side and criticizing it on the other gets us nowhere. In that divisiveness we will never find the spirit of fatherhood that we need both as a society and in our individual lives as men and women.

The Odyssey teaches us that it is a challenge to evoke the deep father and not to be satisfied with substitutes and empty roles. There is no easy route to soul and no simple way of establishing fatherhood. And yet, without the mythic father's guidance and authority, we are left disoriented and out of control. In times of chaos, especially, we might intensify and expand our prayer, speaking it from the heart: "Our father, who art in heaven and who art on the sea, hallowed be thy name."

The Mother

The story, as we find it told in the ancient "Homeric Hymn to Demeter," begins when Persephone, apart from her mother, was picking flowers—roses, crocuses, violets, irises, hyacinths, and narcissi. The earth grew the narcissus as an enchanting lure. It was wonderfully bright, the hymn tells us, and astonished anyone who saw it. It had a hundred heads and a fragrance that pleased the sky, the earth, and the sea.

Persephone was just reaching for the narcissus when the earth opened up and Hades appeared, grabbing her to himself against her will. As he forced her into his golden chariot, she screamed, but no one heard her except the sun and the moon. Zeus was away on business, and besides, the hymn says, he was in favor of the abduction. Finally, Demeter heard her daughter's grieving, and "a sharp pain seized her heart." Immediately, throwing off her headdress and abstaining from divine food and drink, she went off in search of her daughter.

Demeter,
5th c. BCE.

Hades is the "Invisible One," lord of the underworld. His is the realm of essences, the eternal factors that, while they are very much part of life, are invisible. For the Greeks, the underworld was the proper home of the soul, and if we are to have depth and soul, we need some relationship to this underworld, or at least a sense of being partly at home there. Odysseus, as we have already seen, needed to acquaint himself with the underworld as part of his fatherhood. Orpheus also visited the underworld and discovered that it is difficult sometimes to return from it. Jesus, too, journeyed to the land of the dead in the time between his death and resurrection, and Dante began his mystical pilgrimage there. The image of "underworld" in these stories has a relation to actual death, but it also represents the invisible, mysterious, unfathomable depths of a person or a society.

The Persephone myth informs us that sometimes one discovers soul and the underworld against one's will. Certain attractive things in the world may act as lures, setting us up for a challenging fall into the depths of self.

Parents know how easy it is for their children to be attracted to people and activities that are dangerous and that threaten to lead their children into dark places. To the child, antisocial behavior can be fascinating, while to the parent such a thing could destroy all their efforts to give the child a sense of values and a decent path in life. We might understand the story of Persephone as the myth of every child, realizing that the child's susceptibility to dark people and places may be a dangerous but sometimes unavoidable way of soul-making.

Demeter and Persephone are two aspects of the one mythic abduction. Something in us leans toward depth, toying with narcissistic lures, while something else tries to keep us on track, in a world of familiar, wholesome values. Demeter's love of Persephone and her persistence in searching for her allow the daughter to find the land of soul without losing her life altogether. Demeter shows us the ultimate test of the mother: affirming her attachment and her own wishes for her child, while at the same time remaining loyal to her as she goes through a transformative experience.

It is tempting to try to live without an underworld, without soul, and without concern for the mysterious elements that touch on the spiritual and the religious. In the story, when Demeter finds out that Zeus has approved her daughter's abduction, she decides to go into the world as a mortal. She takes an ordinary job as a nanny in a household at Eleusis, a town near Athens.

An infant boy, Demophoön, is put in Demeter's charge, and she cares for him, anointing him with ambrosia, breathing on him, and holding him—strong images of intimate caring for human life on the part of divinity. At night she places him in a fire in order to make him immortal, until his mother sees what is happening and screams out in terror. Demeter becomes very angry at the mortal's failure to understand. "You don't

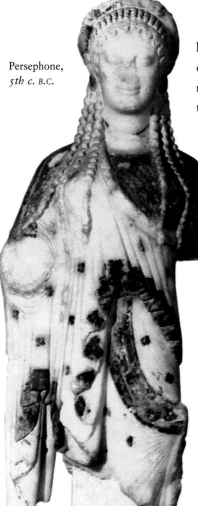

Persephone,
5th c. B.C.

know when fate is bringing you something good or something bad." This is good advice from the mother of mothers: understand that sometimes things that look dangerous from a mortal point of view may be beneficial from a greater perspective.

In her brief term as a mortal nurse, Demeter gives us more lessons in mothering, showing us that motherhood is about nurturing not only in human ways but also in divine ways. Holding the child in fire is a way of burning away the human elements in order to establish immortality. We don't have to take "immortality" to mean literal life after death, but rather the soul's ever-present depth. Good Demeter mothering keeps a child in the heat and passion of life which immortalize and establish soulfulness. Mothering involves not only physical survival and achievement—Demeter's grain and fruit—it is also concerned with guiding a child to his or her unknown depths and the mystery of fate.

The myth of Demeter and Persephone teaches us that mothering is not a simple matter of taking care of the immediate needs of another; it is a recognition that each individual has a special character and fate—qualities of soul—that must be safeguarded even at the risk of losing ordinary assurances of safety and normality. Burning the child in the fire of fate and experience goes against the natural desire for protection. The myth shows us that there is a difference between human mothering and divine mothering. The latter has a broader perspective and is a deep form of the maternal impulse.

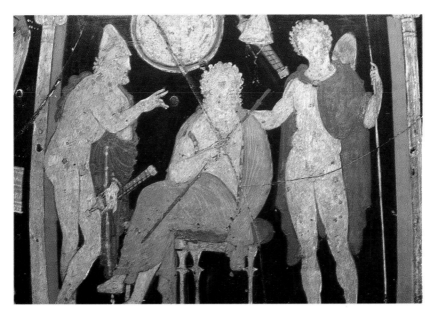

Funerary amphora with Ulysses, Agamemnon and Diomedes.
Mu Archeologico, Florence, Italy.

In the myth, Demeter then shows her divinity and asks that a temple be built in her honor; we go from Demeter as mortal nanny to Demeter as revered goddess. It is precisely at this point in the story—at the end of her role as mortal nursemaid—that Demeter refuses to allow the fields to bear fruit and threatens the extinction of the human race. In ordinary life, when we are being initiated into the mysteries of Demeter—becoming an individual by being seized from deep within—there may be a loss of meaning and fruitfulness in the external world. Ordinarily, Demeter is Mother Nature giving us food and the materials for clothing; she is the goddess of survival needs and of the pleasures of the natural world. But when we find ourselves captured by this myth, these outer benefits may diminish, while inner, underworld activities take precedence.

At this point, because Demeter's suffering is painful to everyone, Zeus is compelled to seek out arbitration, so that there might be some compromise between the legitimate claims of Hades and Demeter's fierce desire to have her daughter back in life. Finally, he

Rape of Europa, *detail of an Etruscan hydria. Second half 6th c. BCE, from Cerveteri.*

dispatches Hermes, the consummate go-between and arbiter, to ask Hades for help.

Hades "smiled grimly and did not disobey the commands of King Zeus." He tells Persephone to return to her mother, but first he secretly puts a pomegranate seed in her mouth, ensuring that she will never be completely free of his realm. She will spend one-third of her time with him, and the rest with her mother.

A student once pointed out to me that these are the proportions of sleeping and waking. At least a third of life, too, seems to belong to the lord of death, as we feel the pain of lost relationships, fading hopes, and failed endeavors.

A way to reconcile these intimations of death with vibrant Demeter life is to turn to Hermes—to "hermeneutics," the art of reading our experiences for their poetry. This Hermes point of view can perceive how our experiences of depth and darkness may be reconciled with ordinary life. According to the myth, Hermes can restore the relationship between the mother-soul, who wants life to thrive no matter what, and the daughter-soul, who has an inclination away from life toward the unknown. With the help of Hermes, we can "see through" our self-destructiveness and depression, our flirtations with danger and our addictions, and ask what they might be accomplishing in our lives and what they are expressing.

The Eleusinian mystery is fundamental because it concerns our very survival, both physical and psychological. We become persons through dangerous experiences of darkness; we can survive these difficult initiations. Any real initiation is always a movement from death to new life. The Eleusinian mystery involves our resurrection—like Persephone, like the appearance of fruit and grain in season—from soul-making depth into continuous, bountiful life. Like Odysseus' wife Penelope weaving a shroud the whole time of the odyssey. Demeter's pain, neurotic activities, and rage accompany, and therefore serve, the soul's visit to the underworld.

Persephone was known as the queen of the underworld and was pictured in art seated on her throne next to Hades. She has an eternal place of honor there, even as she returns to her mother and tells her, as any daughter would, all the details of her abduction. The soul needs to establish itself in the deathly realm, as well as in life.

The wise mother knows that her child can become a person only by living this mystery that was dramatized at Eleusis many centuries ago. We can't hide all the lures that lead us into dissolution. We try in vain to keep our children away from the contamination of death, as we learn from the story of Buddha's parents, who tried to protect him from all human suffering; but full mothering demands that the child be allowed to take the risk.

In the end, Demeter brings back the richness and fullness of nature, and the singer of her hymn reminds us that Hades is also known as Pluto, the god of wealth. Both Demeter and Pluto enrich life, though their harmony most frequently appears as a riddle. The hymn ends with a prayer that is a petition to the most profound mother of all:

Lady, who bears such great gifts,
who brings the seasons,
sovereign, Deo,
you and your very beautiful daughter,
Persephone,
be kind, and, in exchange for my poem,
give me the kind of life my heart wants.

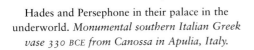

Hades and Persephone in their palace in the underworld. *Monumental southern Italian Greek vase 330 BCE from Canossa in Apulia, Italy.*

The Child

At the beginning of midnight Mass in the Roman Catholic church the choir chants, *"Puer natus est nobis."* "A child is born to us." Christmas is the celebration of Jesus as infant and divinity entering the human arena. This motif of the divine child is common to many religions, suggesting not only the childhood of the God, but also the divinity of childhood. Just as the mythic mother is a foundational principle of all life, so the divine child is an aspect of all experience. Jung, inspired by mythological stories of heroes' childhoods, described the child of the soul, the archetypal child, as everything that is abandoned, exposed, vulnerable, and yet divinely powerful. Once again we find the richness of paradox, a Janus-faced archetype of both power and weakness in play at the same moment.

Mythology from many cultures tells of the special child, abandoned by its parents, raised in the wild or by lowly foster parents. There is, in fact,

Virgin and Child,
15th c. Ferrarese walnut polychrome figure.

an aspect of the child that is utterly exposed to fate, time, and conditions—not protected by being in a more personal context. Yet, this exposure is what allows the child to become someone new and powerful. Our own exposure to life is both a threat and an opportunity. In those moments when we feel particularly vulnerable, that child might appear as both defenseless and ready to be prepared for a special role in life.

Some modern psychologies see the "child within" as a figure of creativity and spontaneity. But Jung's child is more complex. We approach the power of this child not by fleeing its vulnerability, but by claiming it. There is a special power associated with the very ignorance and incapacity of the child figure. Children often appear in dreams wandering down a city street, abandoned, not knowing where to go or how to get help. This is a condition of the soul's childhood. We may be tempted, upon awakening from such a dream, to resolve never to be so lost and disoriented. But if we are going to acknowledge the child and care for this figure, too, without trying to "improve" upon it, then we have to find a place for wandering, dislocation, and helplessness. These, too, are the child.

Every day we use phrases that subtly speak against the child. "I'm being very immature," a person will say self-critically about the expression of some primitive feeling. If you can make that statement without its being a criticism of the child, simply as a matter of fact, then it may be an accurate description of the myth that is being lived at the moment. I am being immature. Immaturity is part of my nature.

Or we might say, "This is an old problem, going back to childhood." Again, we think of childhood as something to grow out of. It is the cause of all present trouble. If only it had been different! But this rejection of the child is another way to reject oneself and certainly not to care for the soul. That child who is eternally present in our thoughts and dreams may be full of weakness and faults, but that is who we are.

The child's unknowing is also fertile. In the Gospel, the child Jesus is separated from his parents on a trip to Jerusalem, and he is found discussing points of theology with the rabbis in the temple. Is this a miracle story, or is it a reminder of the special intelligence of the child, so unformed and yet, as Jung says, so wise? Nicholas of Cusa, the great fifteenth-century theologian who wrote a book about the importance of "educated ignorance," says we have to find ways to unlearn those things that screen us from the perception of profound truth. We have to *achieve* the child's unknowing because we have been made so smart. Zen also recommends not losing the "beginner's mind," so important for immediacy in experience.

I suspect, further, that if we could come to appreciate the archetypal child whom we feel within ourselves, we might have a more open and appreciative relationship to actual children. For example, an eternal question about children is, how should we educate them? *Education* means "to lead out." We seem to understand this as leading away from childhood, but maybe we could think of it as eliciting the wisdom and the talents of childhood itself. As A. S. Neal, founder of the Summerhill School, taught many years ago, we can trust that the child already has talents and intelligence. Child wisdom is different from adult wisdom, but it has its place.

In his memoirs Jung makes a remarkable statement about the child. Childhood, he says, "sketches a more complete picture of the self, of the whole man in his pure individuality, than adulthood." He goes on to say that a child will arouse primitive longings in an adult for unfulfilled desires that have been lost in adaptation to civilization. We have been seduced into the myth of progress, so that at the social level we assume that we are more intelligent and more developed than our ancestors, and at the personal level we assume that adults are more intelligent than children. This developmental fantasy runs deep, affecting many of our values. We live in a hierarchical world in which we defend ourselves from our primitive nature by looking down on less developed cultures, and from our eternal infancy and childhood by insisting on a graded, necessary elevation through learning and technological sophistication out of the child into the adult. This is not a true initiation that values both the previous form of existence and the newly attained one; it is a defense against the humiliating reality of the child, a humility that embarrasses the Promethean longing for adult control of life but nevertheless is full of soul. We are not caring for the soul when we fabricate ways of denying its inferior stations, childhood prominent among them. We care for the soul by acknowledging the place of eternal childhood, seeing its disadvantages to be virtuous and its inadequacies to be the conduits of soulful sensitivity.

Enigma dell'ora *by Georgio de Chirico, 1912.*

CHAPTER THREE

Self-love and Its Myth:
Narcissus and Narcissism

MAINSTREAM PSYCHOLOGY PUTS A GREAT DEAL OF FAITH in a strong ego. Ego development and positive self-concept are considered important ingredients of a mature personality. Yet narcissism, the habit of focusing attention on oneself rather than the world of objects and of others, is considered a disorder. On the other hand, Jungian psychology, with its emphasis on the unconscious, and archetypal psychology, with its high regard for the non-ego personalities of the psyche, give the impression that the ego is a sinner, literalizing all over the place and generally making a mess. Add religion's longstanding warnings against selfishness and self-love, in which pride is considered one of the cardinal sins, and it begins to look as though there is a moral conspiracy against the ego.

The one-sidedness and moralism of the various attacks on narcissism suggest that there may be some soul lying around in this rejected pile of ego and self-love: anything that bad must have some value in it. Could it be that our righteous rejections of narcissism and love of self cover over a mystery about the nature of the soul's loves? Is our negative branding of narcissism a defense against a demanding call of the soul to be loved?

The problem is not just theoretical. I'm often surprised in my therapeutic work when an otherwise mature and discerning adult

Narcissus and Echo by Nicholas Poussin.

who is faced with some tough choice collapses everything into the statement "I can't be selfish." When I explore this weighty moral imperative with the person further, I usually find that it is tied to a religious upbringing. "I was taught never to be self- ish," she will say with finality. I notice, however, that while this person insists on her selflessness, she seems in fact to be quite preoccupied with herself.

Our common intolerance for narcissism in another is an indication that there is sand in that particular oyster; our reaction is a signal that this area may hold something of importance. In this sense, narcissism is a shadow quality. Jung explains that when we meet something of the shadow in another, we often feel repulsed, but that is because we are confronting something in ourselves that we find objectionable, something with which we ourselves struggle, and something that contains qualities valuable to the soul. The nega- tive image we have of narcissism may indicate that self-preoccupation contains something we need so badly that it is surrounded with negative connotations. Our irritated moralism keeps it at bay, but also signals us that soul is present.

How, then, do we preserve the symptom of narcissism, assuming that there is a gold nugget in that clump of dirt? How do we penetrate through the superficial sludge to the deeper necessity? The answer, as we are beginning to recognize by now, is to bring the wisdom of the imagination into play. In the case of narcissism, the path is clearly laid out: we can study the myth of Narcissus, after whom the disorder is named.

Narcissus

The ancient story of Narcissus, as told in the *Metamorphoses* of the Roman writer Ovid, is not just a simple story of a boy falling in love with himself. It has many subtle, telling details. Ovid tells us, for instance, that Narcissus was the son of a river god and a nymph. In mythology, parentage can often be taken as holding poetic truths. Apparently there is something essentially liquid or watery about Narcissus, and by extension, about our own narcissism. When we are narcissistic, we are not on solid ground (earth) or thinking clearly (air) or caught up in passion (fire). Somehow, if we follow the myth, we are dreamlike, fluid, not clearly formed, more immersed in a stream of fantasy than secure in a firm identity.

Another detail that appears at the opening of the story is the prophecy of Tiresias, the renowned seer: "He will live to a ripe old age," he pronounces about Narcissus, "provided he never comes to know himself." This is a strange foretelling: it indicates that the story is about knowing oneself as well as loving oneself and that self-knowledge will lead to death.

The next we hear of him, Narcissus is sixteen and so lovely that many young people are attracted to him; but he is filled with a "hard pride," Ovid says, and no one can truly get through to him. One nymph who falls in love with him, Echo, has her own peculiar qualities: she can only speak words and phrases she has just heard from someone else. One day Narcissus loses sight of his friends and cries out, "Is anyone here?"

"Here," Echo answers.

"Let's meet here," Narcissus says.

"Meet here," Echo responds. When she approaches him, Narcissus backs away.

"I would die before I would give my power to you," he says.

"I would give my power to you," she says in her own way. In her grief, feeling rejected and frustrated, Echo then loses her body and becomes a mere voice.

In this early episode we see Narcissus before he has attained self-knowledge. He presents an image of narcissism that has not yet found its mystery. Here we see the symptom: a self-absorption and containment that allow no connections of the heart. The echoing aspect of narcissism—the feeling that everything in the world is only a reflection of oneself—doesn't want to give away power. To respond to another or to an object in the outside world would endanger the fragile sense of power which that tight, defensive insistence on oneself maintains. Like all symptomatic behavior, narcissism reveals, in the very things it insists on, exactly what it lacks. In other words, the narcissist's *display* of self-love is in itself a sign that he can't find a way adequately to love himself.

In Jungian language we could recognize the *puer* or boyish side of the psyche in Narcissus—distant, cold, self-contained. Echo is the anima, the soul in desperate need of attachment to the boyish beauty. But in the presence of Narcissus the soul shrivels into an echoing voice.

One of the young people scorned by Narcissus offers a curse: "May he fall in love and not have what he loves." The goddess Nemesis hears the prayer and decides to answer it. Narcissus is about to have a transforming, life-threatening, psychotic episode at a pool of water. The intervention of a god, however, may signal a breaking up of symptomatic behavior, the neurosis beginning to dissolve in painful disorientation. The divine breaking up of narcissism may be expected to center on self-knowledge and self-love.

The young man approaches a pool of water, so still and smooth that it has never been disturbed by either human or animal. It is surrounded by a cool, dark grove of trees. As Narcissus puts his head to the water to get a drink, he sees his image in the water and his attention is frozen. Like the young people who desired him before, Narcissus feels a great yearning to possess this form. He reaches into the water, but he can't get hold of it. "What you are looking for," says Ovid, "is nowhere. Turn your head away and what you love will be lost."

Here we see the beginning of the symptom's fulfillment. Narcissism, that absorption in oneself that is soulless and loveless, turns gradually into a deeper version of itself. It becomes a true stillness, a wonder about oneself, a meditation on one's nature. For the first time the narcissist reflects—a major image in the story—on himself. Formerly, his preoccupation with himself was empty, but now it stirs wonder. In symptomatic narcissism there is no reflection and no wonder. But now, as it undergoes transformation into a deeper version of itself, the narcissism takes on more substance.

The story then tells how Narcissus feels the longing to be united with the image he has found. He talks to the trees, saying, "Has anyone ever had as much longing as I have?" Talking to nature shows that his grief is giving him a new connection to the soul. When soul is present, nature is alive.

James Hillman has written about longing as an important activity of the soul, especially the young soul, *puer*. That which is young in us pines and yearns. It feels separation keenly and painfully desires attachment. So, the myth suggests that we are on our way toward healing narcissism when we feel an overwhelming desire to be the person we newly imagine ourselves to be. Nations, as well as individuals, can go through this initiation. America has a great longing to *be* the New World of opportunity and a moral beacon for the world. It longs to fulfill these narcissistic images of itself. At the same time it is painful to realize the distance between the reality and that image. America's narcissism is strong. It is paraded before the world. If we were to put the nation on the couch, we might discover that narcissism is its most obvious symptom. America's narcissism is its unrefined *puer* spirit of genuine new vision.

Narcissus lies at the edge of the pool tormented by the realization that this boy in the water is separated from him by the thinnest membrane. He is in the midst of these thoughts when a realization strikes him suddenly. "It's me!" he says in profound surprise. Up to this point he did not know that the face he loved so much was his own.

Echo by Alfred Gatley, 1816–1863.

This is a key point in the story. Narcissus falls in love with a person in a watery mirror who he thinks is someone else, even though it is himself. Narcissism gets stuck on certain familiar images of self. We love the surface image we identify as ourselves, but Narcissus discovers by accident that there are other images just as lovable. They are in the pool, at the very source of identity. The cure for narcissism, certainly a way of caring for the soul, is to be open to these other images. Narcissism, like the neurotic Narcissus, is hard and impenetrable. But Narcissus at the pool recovers his natural moisture. As with the flower, he has become flexible, beautiful, planted.

A subtle point: Narcissus becomes able to love himself only when he learns to love that self as an object. He now has a view of himself as someone else. This is not ego loving ego; this is ego loving the soul, loving a face the soul presents. We might say that the cure for narcissism is to move from love of self, which always has a hint of narcissism in it, to love of one's deep soul.

Discovering that the face in the pool is his own, Narcissus exclaims, "What I long for I have." Love of a new image of self leads to new knowledge about oneself and one's potential.

Narcissus begins to entertain thoughts of death. "Now grief is sapping my strength," he says, "and only a brief space of life remains for me. I am cut off in life's prime." We are led to a mystery that is embedded in all initiations

Narcissus and Echo *by John William Waterhouse, 1849–1917.*

and in every rite of passage: the end of a previous form of existence is felt as a real death.

Images of dying may attend movements in our own narcissism: that hard-shelled boy has to surrender his existence. The only way through our narcissism is to feel the mortal wound, an end to the I-project we have set up and maintained with such attention.

The Narcissus myth can be lived in many ways. Sometimes the pool may appear in another person. In that person I might recognize an image I could love and be. But such chance encounters with an image that is at once both me and not-me are dangerous. Life may never again be the same. The "I" I have been may quickly deteriorate and succumb to the process of self-transformation. Narcissism is like a carrot leading us through life from one desirable "self" to another.

Ovid next shifts his imagery to the element fire. First Narcissus strikes his chest in grief, and his skin "takes on a delicate glow," like the flush of an apple. Narcissus is consumed by the hidden fire of love. Love's fire chases the chill that had been characteristic of the old Narcissus. Theological commentaries on this tale used it as moral evidence against self-love, but in fact the story shows that love is the transforming factor. Warming love creates soul.

The story in Ovid ends with a colorful detail. His companions look for his body but cannot find it. In its place they find a flower with a yellow center and white petals. Here we see the hard, rigid marble narcissism transformed into the soft, flexible textures of a daffodil, the narcissus. Care of the soul requires us to see the myth in the symptom, to know that there is a flower waiting to break through the hard surface of narcissism. Knowing the mythology, we are able to embrace the symptom, glimpsing something of the mysterious rule by which a disease of the psyche can be its own cure.

Narcissism and Polytheism

The story of Narcissus makes it clear that one of the dangers of narcissism is its inflexibility and rigidity. Suppleness is an extremely important quality of soul.

In Greek mythology, the flexibility of the gods and goddesses is one of their primary traits. They may fight each other, but they recognize each other's validity. Each of the gods and goddesses has a particular way of sustaining the polytheism of their arrangement.

Polytheism understood as a psychological model rather than a religious belief is easily misunderstood. Stated simply, it means that psychologically we have many different claims made on us from a deep place. It is not possible, nor is it desirable, to get all of these impulses together under a single focus. Rather than strive for unity of personality, the idea of polytheism suggests living within multiplicity.

The most rewarding quality of polytheism is the intimacy it can make possible with one's own heart. When we try to keep life in order with a monotheistic attitude— do the right thing, keep up the traditions, and be sure that life makes sense—our moralism against ourselves can keep certain parts of our nature at a distance and little known.

An attitude of polytheism permits a degree of acceptance of human nature and of one's own nature that is otherwise blocked by single-mindedness. A neurotic narcissism won't allow the time needed to stop, reflect, and see the many emotions, memories, wishes, fantasies, desires, and fears that make up the materials of the soul. As a result, the narcissistic person becomes fixed on a single idea of who he is, and other possibilities are automatically rejected. We can read the myth, especially the discovery of the "other" face in the pool, as a lesson in polytheism.

We can see narcissism, then, as an opportunity rather than as a problem: not a personality defect, but the soul trying to find its otherness. Narcissism is less a simple focus on ego and more a

Kouros of Piraeus, *bronze 500 BCE.*

manifestation of the need for a paradoxical sense of self, one that includes both the ego and the non-ego.

The Flowering of Life

Some years ago, when I was teaching psychology at a state university, a bright, interesting young man came into one of my classes. He seemed quite mature: he was dedicated to social issues and he liked to discuss ideas. He even read serious books on his own, something rather unusual in this school. But I could also sense early Narcissus in him, a way he had of drawing people around him and yet keeping a distance. Echo was there, too. He had a habit of repeating many ideas he had heard from several sources as though they were his own—one of the telltale signs of narcissism. But I didn't realize how much he was fated toward the myth until one day he asked to have a private talk with me.

He sat across from me looking uncharacteristically serious.

"What's up?" I asked.

"I have to tell somebody," he said with fire in his eyes, "what has happened to me."

"Go on," I said.

"I have discovered something about myself."

"Yes."

"I'm Jesus Christ."

"Oh," I said. I wasn't prepared for such a stark expression of his self-esteem.

"I have a mission to save the world," he went on. "I know I can perform miracles, and in case you get me wrong, I don't mean I am a Christian or a follower of Jesus or Christlike. I am Jesus himself come back to earth. I know it sounds crazy, but it's true."

I believe this young man did indeed have a strong calling in his life. He had talent, conviction, idealism, and energy. But certainly, if his symptomatic narcissism never deepened, he would be in trouble. He would never be able to accomplish anything in the world, and at best he might be condemned to a life of frustrated ideal-

Wanderer looking over a Sea of Fog *by Caspar David Friedrich, 1815.*

Les yeux Clos *by Odilon Redon, 1905.*

ism. I thought my student's potential for real life was as great as his narcissistic fantasies were absurd. For him, care of the soul would mean tending these fantasies, nurturing them until they coalesced into power and effectiveness.

Some psychologists argue that the soaring, idealistic *puer* cries out for grounding. He needs to be pulled down to where the rest of us live. But I have doubts about such a compensatory move into an opposite attitude. It could maintain the split and completely confuse the individual so caught up in flights of fantasy. We could take a more homeopathic approach, accepting what is given in the symptom while at the same time deepening it.

In the myth, Narcissus's own nature flowers, literally. He doesn't become a mature adult full of remorse for his adolescent foolishness. In fact, the motif of the boy in the underworld eternally meditating on his image suggests that narcissism is healed when it is invited into the very essence of the personality and when that youthful spirit becomes lodged eternally in the soul.

Often we are blocked from seeing a possible positive outcome in narcissism because it generates such strong shadow feelings. It goes against one of the professed virtues of American culture: humility. We are supposed to be humble and unassuming. Narcissism is the shadow of that humility, and so we try to pull it down to an acceptable level. But narcissism, even at a social level, suggests that what we need is not humility, especially the false kind that arises from the repression of ambition, but great dreams, high ideals, and pleasure in our own talent and abilities.

The solution to narcissism is not "growing up." On the contrary, the solution to narcissism is to give the myth as much realization as possible, to the point where a tiny bud appears indicating the flowering of personality through its narcissism.

Self-love

Narcissism is a condition in which a person does *not* love himself. This failure in love comes through as its opposite because the person tries so hard to find self-acceptance. The complex reveals itself in the all-too-obvious effort and exaggeration.

It's clear to all around that narcissism's love is shallow. We know instinctively that someone who talks about himself all the time must not have a very strong sense of self. To the individual caught up in this myth, the failure to find self-love is felt as a kind of masochism, and, whenever masochism comes into play, a sadistic element is not far behind. The two attitudes are polar elements in a split power archetype.

The narcissist is clearly sadistic in his rejection of others and in his feelings of superiority. Masochism, on the other hand, appears with particular clarity in what I call "negative narcissism." One time an artist was talking to me about her painting. She showed me samples of her work, and it seemed to me that she was very educated and could well devote her life to art. But as we talked, I noticed that something in her attitude toward herself and her work interfered.

"I particularly like the realism without perspective in your recent paintings," I said.

"Oh, I don't know," she said. "I think it just shows that I haven't studied enough. You know, I always wanted to go to art school, but my family could never afford to send me."

"How do you manage to make those colors look so harmonious and yet filled with contrast, all at the same time?" I asked, truly taken by her style.

"I'm not really trained in these things," she went on, with her concern about her background and pedigree.

Putting oneself down is narcissism in reverse. It robs the soul of its attachment to the world. This woman wasn't attached to her work because of her overriding concern with her image. I suspect that if she had an image of herself as an artist, and loved it, she would be able to forget about her inferior feelings about herself and concentrate on her work. Soul always includes an element of attachment, but narcissism, as we have seen from the myth, is the failure to make oneself available for attachment.

The healing of narcissism, the fulfillment of its symptomatic hunger, is achieved by giving the ego what it needs—pleasure in accomplishment, acceptance, and some degree of recognition. Masochistic refusal of the ego's desire is no way to care for the soul. On the contrary, it is an ascetic bargain that buys a false sense of virtue

Narcissus *by Gustav Moreau, 1895.*

at the cost of the soul's need. Motivated by thoughts of purity and self-control, a person can deny the ego all kinds of comforts, and yet narcissism may abound. Spiritual programs are filled with concerns for individual progress, acceptance by authorities, and the wish for sainthood or some other high position. An alternative approach is to hear the soul's complaint and give it love and attention where it most needs it, even where we are most suspicious.

The secret in healing narcissism is not to heal it at all, but to listen to it. Narcissism is a signal that the soul is not being loved sufficiently. Narcissus falls in love with his image, but he doesn't know it is he that is loved. He discovers by his own experience that he is lovable. Further, he loves himself as an object. In our age of personalism and subjectivity it is considered a sin to make a person into an object.

Yet that is the only way to see ourselves objectively. We can examine the stuff of our lives and personalities as material separate from the "I." I am stuff. I am made up of things and qualities, and in loving these things I love myself.

When we recognize the objective nature of the soul, so that we may love it without becoming caught in solipsistic self-absorption, we can love ourselves as Narcissus did, as Other.

The myth also teaches us something else: that narcissism is a piece in a larger scheme of transformation. In the story, the scene shifts from woods to underworld, the character from human to flower, that is, from person to object. I see in this a movement away from human subjectivity and into nature. Narcissism heals itself away from loneliness into creation: in our narcissism we wound nature and make things that cannot be loved, but when our narcissism is transformed, the result is the love of self that engenders a sense of union with all of nature and things. You might say that we then have a shared narcissism, a mutual self-love, a kind of mystical consanguinity among all creatures. Not shying away from mysticism, we might say that symptomatic narcissism can only be healed when it becomes a genuine religious virtue. All human symptoms and problems, when they are taken to their depth and realized in a soulful way, find their ultimate solution in a religious sensibility.

Rainer Maria Rilke was the poet of this philosophy of transforming the everyday into the sacred, the visible into the invisible. In a famous letter of 1925 he writes, "Our task is to stamp this provisional, perishing earth into ourselves so deeply, so painfully and passionately, that its being may rise again, `invisibly,' in us." This

reminds me of Narcissus becoming the flower: nature manifests itself through our human lives, and our personalities flower as acts of creation. In his *Sonnets to Orpheus* Rilke again refers plainly to Narcissus:

> *Though the reflection in the pool*
> *Often swims before our eyes:*
> *Know the image.*
> *Only in the dual realm*
> *do voices become*
> *eternal and mild.*

The trouble is that all too often our symptoms go unworked. Metamorphosis doesn't happen without our artful participation. This is the teaching of the Renaissance magicians like Ficino and Pico della Mirandola, who wrote that we need to be the artists and poets of our own lives. Symptoms are transformed by imagination. If I hear a bit of narcissism shoot out of my mouth, I can take the clue and look for those places where I am not loving and tending my soul. The circumstances, the timing, and the particular language of my narcissism tell me exactly where to look and what to do. Oddly, I can be thankful for my narcissism, if I recognize it as such and hear within it the rumblings of myth. It contains the seeds of self-acceptance and a loving attachment to the broad world.

CHAPTER FOUR

Love's Initiations

LOVE IS A KIND OF MADNESS, PLATO SAID, A DIVINE MADNESS. **Today we talk** about love as though it were primarily an aspect of relationship and also, to a great degree, as if it were something within our control. We're concerned about how to do it right, how to make it successful, how to overcome its problems, and how to survive its failures. Many of the problems people bring to therapy involve the high expectations and the rock-bottom experiences of love. It is clear that love is never simple, that it brings with it struggles of the past and hopes for the future, and that it is loaded with material that may be remotely—if at all—connected to the person who is the apparent object of love.

We sometimes talk about love lightly, not acknowledging how powerful and lasting it can be. We always expect love to be healing and whole, and then are astonished to find that it can create hollow gaps and empty failures. In his *Symposium*, his great book on the nature of love, Plato called love the child of fullness and emptiness. Each of these aspects somehow accompanies the other.

Our love of love and our high expectations that it will somehow make life complete seem to be an integral part of the experience. Love seems to promise that life's gaping wounds will close up and heal. It makes little difference that in the past love has shown itself to be painful and disturbing. There is something self-renewing in love. Like the goddesses of Greece, it is able to renew its virginity in a bath of forgetfulness.

Il Bacio *by Francesco Hayez, 1791-1881.*

Carl Gustav Jung.

I suppose we do learn some things about love each time we experience it. In the failure of a relationship we resolve never to make the same mistakes again. We get toughened to some extent and perhaps become a little wiser. But love itself is eternally young and always manifests some of the folly of youth. So, maybe it is better not to become too jaded by love's suffering and dead ends, but rather to appreciate that emptiness is part of love's heritage and therefore its very nature.

It may be useful to consider love less as an aspect of relationship and more as an event of the soul. This is the point of view taken in ancient handbooks. There is no talk about making relationships work, although there is celebration of friendship and intimacy. The emphasis is on what love does to the soul. Does it bring broader vision? Does it initiate the soul in some way? Does it carry the lover away from earth to an awareness of divine things?

Ficino says, "What is human love? What is its purpose? It is the desire for union with a beautiful object in order to make eternity available to mortal life." It is a fundamental teaching of the Neoplatonists that earthly pleasures are an invitation to eternal delights. Ficino says that these things of ordinary life that enchant us toward eternity are "magical decoys." In other words, what appears to be a fully earthly relationship between two human individuals is at the same time a path toward far deeper experiences of the soul. Love confuses its victims because its work in the soul does not always coincide in every detail with the apparent tempos and requirements of relationship. The early Romantic German poet Novalis put it quite simply: love, he says, was not made for this world.

Freud offers one way of turning our focus in love away from the contingencies of life and toward the soul. He says that love always involves a transference to the present relationship of early family patterns. Father, mother, brother, and sister are always implicated in love as invisible but influential presences. Freud turns our attention toward deeper fantasies that wake into action when love stirs.

We can understand Freud to be reminding us that love ushers in a whole community of people. I recall a dream I had about fifteen years ago. I was in a large bedroom with a beautiful woman whom I didn't know from life. I wanted to turn off the bright lights, which were a distraction. I found a long light switch on the wall with about twenty buttons on it. As I pressed one, some lights would go out and others would go on. I pushed and pushed those buttons, but I couldn't achieve the

Sigmund Freud.

darkness I wanted. Finally I gave up, and then crowds of people began to come into the bedroom. It was hopeless. I couldn't have the darkness or the privacy I craved.

There is something about being in love that wishes for blindness, pure absorption and freedom from complexity. In that dream I didn't want all the other figures of the soul to have any part in this opportunity for plain, unadulterated love. Nor did I want any light. I wanted pure unconsciousness, absolute darkness.

I once worked with a woman who was about to be married. During that time she had a series of disturbing dreams in which her brother kept interfering with her wedding. He was in love with her, and he was determined to destroy this marriage that would end his intimacy with his sister. The woman told me she also had waking images about loving her brother and wishing she could marry both him and her fiancé. What was particularly interesting about the intensity of her feelings was that in life she had no brother. He was a strong, active, interfering figure of her soul. Apparently he was giving her the opportunity to reflect and question. In Jungian terms, he acted as a valuable animus figure, offering criticism and pause. In his essay on marriage, Jung says that love always involves four persons: the person, the lover, the anima and the animus.

Eros and Psyche. *Roman copy after
a Hellenistic original, 2nd c.* BCE.

A general principle we can take from Freud is that love sparks imagination into extraordinary activity. Being "in love" is like being "in imagination." The literal concerns of everyday life, yesterday such a preoccupation, now practically disappear in the rush of love's daydreams. Concrete reality recedes as the imaginal world settles in. Thus, the "divine madness" of love is akin to the mania of paranoia and other dissociations.

Love releases us into the realm of divine imagination, where the soul is expanded and reminded of its unearthly cravings and needs. We think that when a lover inflates his loved one he is failing to acknowledge her flaws—"Love is blind." But it may be the other way around. Love allows a person to see the true angelic nature of another person, the halo, the aureole of divinity. Certainly from the perspective of ordinary life this is madness and illusion. But if we let loose our hold on our philosophies and psychologies of enlightenment and reason, we might learn to appreciate the perspective of eternity that enters life as madness, Plato's divine frenzy.

Love brings consciousness closer to the dream state. In that sense, it may reveal more than it distorts, as a dream reveals—poetically, suggestively, and, admittedly, obscurely. If we were to appreciate truly the Platonic theory of love, we might also learn to see other forms of madness, such as paranoia and addiction, as evidence of the soul's reaching toward its proper yearnings. Platonic love is not love without sex. It is love that finds in the body and in human relationship a route toward eternity. In his book on love, *Convivium*—his answer to Plato's *Symposium*—Ficino, who is credited with coining the phrase "Platonic love," says concisely, "The soul is partly in eternity and partly in time." Love straddles these two dimensions, opening a way to live in both simultaneously. But incursions of eternity into life are usually unsettling, for they disturb our plans and shake the tranquillity we have achieved with earthly reason.

Tristan and Isolde

In order to appreciate the *mystery* of love, we have to give up the idea that love is a psychological problem and that with enough reading and guidance we can finally do it right, without illusion and folly. We do not care for the soul by shrinking it down to reasonable size. Our era's preoccupation with mental hygiene encourages us to think of all forms of mania as disease. But Plato's divine madness is not pathological in our hygienic sense, but more an opening into eternity. It is a relief from the stringent limits of pragmatic, sanitized life. It is a door that opens out from human reason into divine mystery.

The great love stories in our Western tradition help us meditate on the eternal dimensions of love. Showing the many sides of love, they include the Passion of Jesus ("passion" has rich multiple meanings), the Creation in Genesis, the Homecoming of Odysseus, the Melancholy of Hamlet, and the Star-crossed Fate of Tristan and Isolde.

The last is particularly poignant and relevant to our theme. It is a story about love's sadness. The lover's name, Tristan, means sad—*triste*. Like many heroes of legend and mythology, he was raised by a second set of parents; in fact, his mother's brother, King Mark, later adopted him as his son, so all told he had three fathers. We can see this multiple parentage as a sign of special fate, a soul exposed in an unusual way to the vagaries of life.

At first Tristan is a typical young man. Gottfried von Strassburg, author of one of the classic versions of the story, describes Tristan as talented in music, languages, rituals of the hunt, games, and conversation. Whenever he traveled to new lands, he quickly learned the local language, made up convincing tall stories of his adventures, sang enchanting songs, and won the hearts of the people. The tale of Tristan and Isolde, therefore, is about love entering the tragic side of life from this glowing *puer* place: our boyish spirit, relying on its own naïveté and talent, falls into complicated, entangling, overwhelming love.

A telling leitmotif in the story of Tristan is the image of water. His adventures begin when he is playing chess with visiting Norwegian sailors on a ship in the harbor. They abduct him and sail off with him. A storm rises, and to appease the storm gods they send him off alone in a skiff. He arrives in Ireland and meets the queen and her daughter Isolde. He lies to them about who he really is, changing his name to Tantris. He doesn't want them to know that one of the enemies he once killed was Isolde's uncle. But while he is sitting in a bathtub, Isolde discovers his identity and solves the riddle of his name. The scene is a kind of baptism, a christening of the love of the two young people.

Tristan is the epitome of talent and cleverness, whose identity is revealed most clearly when he is adrift or in water, always newly born, eternally young, free of the limitations of pragmatic life. Sometimes when I hear a man or woman tell a dream

Tristan and Isolde from 15th c. Illuminated Manuscript.

of floating in a lake or sitting in a bathtub I think of Tristan. He is not a swimmer; he is always contained in a vessel in the water, but he is also always drifting, having no ordinary practical means of control and safety. His technology in the water is aesthetic and spiritual. He is extremely vulnerable as he drifts toward his fate, yet he enjoys the confidence of his own abilities and his aesthetic contact with the laws of life. He is fluid but not wet.

Unknowingly, Tristan and Isolde drink a love potion the queen has made for Tristan's Uncle Mark, and the second half of their story concerns their dangerous attempts to be illicit lovers in a threatening, castigating world. Their love is too strong to be undone by obligation or social propriety, yet it can never be secure and protected. It ends unfulfilled in the tragic death of the lovers. Like an ever-present shadow, sadness accompanies every thrill and success the two young people squeeze from fate.

If we see Tristan as a figure of our sadness in love, and not as a literal representative of its absolute failure, then we have an image that respects love's dark depths as well as its brilliant heights. When love's sadness visits us, that is Tristan floating on his skiff, trusting and yet moving ever closer to the tragic side of life that redeems his light spirit. It isn't necessary to take a pill or search out a therapeutic strategy to dismiss the feeling, because to dismiss that feeling is to banish an important soul visitor. The soul apparently needs amorous sadness. It is a form of consciousness that brings its own unique wisdom.

Failure, Loss, and Separation

When we read the tale of Tristan and Isolde as myth, we are guided toward reflecting on failure and complexity as part of love, not as something foreign to it. We are also led to a less literal view of separation and loss. The thought of separating enters the minds of many people living a pact of love. But the thought is not the same as literal action. The idea of separation might suggest many things about the love, but the act means only one thing: the destruction of the relationship in its current form.

A sensitive, thoughtful, well-meaning woman, Marianne, once came to me with one idea in mind. "I need to separate from my husband," she said with pain on her face, "and I don't know if I can do it."

"What's going on?" I asked.

"He's a wonderful person," she said. "I love him, and I respect him. But I have an overwhelming need to get away from him. We argue a lot, and our sex life has hit rock bottom. We have three children, and he's a great father. But my need to separate is stronger than my concern for my kids."

I noticed that she used the word "separation" over and over.

Jung talks about separation as an activity of the soul in his studies on medieval alchemy. *Separatio* was an operation the alchemists considered essential to the process of turning ordinary materials into gold. To him *separatio* was a breaking into parts of materials in the psyche that needed differentiation. They were perhaps too tightly packed and couldn't be known for what they were individually. Paracelsus understood *separatio* as the primary activity in creation, both in the creation of the world and in every human creative act. These antique notions were in the back of my mind when I listened to Marianne refer to her desire to separate.

As we talked, it became clear that Marianne had other stories about strong identifications from which she had attempted freeing herself. Her parents, for instance, were overbearing for her and wouldn't let her live her own life.

She talked about the desire she had had at the beginning of her marriage to create her own family, separate from her parents and be free of their influence. But again and again, through their financial support, her parents found their way into the center of her family. She also seemed unconscious of the extent to which she didn't allow her husband his own individuality, but rather acted toward him the way her parents did toward her. All in all, it appeared to me that she needed many kinds of separation in many parts of her life, and especially, of course, in her way of being with others. As for her own psyche, she seemed to crave a release of her spirit from the imprisonment she had felt for many years.

One day Marianne came to tell me that she had decided to move out. She was going to make the separation real, she said.

She moved out, got a new job, and made new friends. She dated a few men and generally enjoyed her new freedom. She was surprised to discover that her husband adjusted well to the new arrangement, and for the first time in years she began to have some feelings of jealousy. She tasted life outside the childhood pattern. Her parents, of course, objected strongly to the separation, but for her this was an added benefit. It pleased her to go against their values and approval. She had married young, and for the first time in her life she found out what it was like to be relatively single and independent, and she liked it. She saw and felt herself in new ways.

After three months of *separatio*, she decided to go back to her home and husband. Several years later she is thriving in that home and is no longer plagued with thoughts of leaving her relationship.

Marianne's story gives us an example of the way that caring for the soul's messages can take us to unexpected places. Separation ideas seem to be opposed to love and marriage, but maybe they are a part of it, the underside, which can be accepted with imagination without destroying the love. Love asks many things of us, including actions that seem to be utterly counter to feelings of attachment and loyalty. Yet these shadow qualities may ultimately bring the love to its proper, if mysterious and unpredictable, home.

Love's Shadows

Unless we deal with the shadow of love, our experience of it will be incomplete. A sentimental philosophy of love, embracing only the romantic and the positive, fails at the first sign of shadow—thoughts of separation, the loss of faith and hope in the relationship, or unexpected changes in the partners' values. Such a partial view also presents impossible ideals and expectations. If love can't match these ideals, it is destroyed for being inadequate. I like to keep in mind that in the heritage of our literature and art, love is portrayed as a child, often with eyes blindfolded, or

Kecyma pſaru contemplat² priaz de orto

Queen in her Tower, *15th c. Flanders.*

The Birthday *by Marc Chagall, 1915.*

as an unruly adolescent. By nature love feels inadequate, but this inadequacy rounds out the wide range of love's emotions. Love finds its soul in its feelings of incompleteness, impossibility, and imperfection.

The Greeks told a strange story of dark love. Admetus was a distinguished man who had been granted a special favor by Apollo because he had helped the god in a time of trouble. As a reward, he was given a way to sidestep death. When death came to take him to the underworld, Admetus was allowed to find someone willing to take his place and die for him. He asked his mother and father, both of whom had lived long happy lives, to die in his place. But they refused, offering reasonable excuses. His wife, Alkestis, however, agreed and went off with Death. By coincidence, at this time the hero Herakles happened to be visiting, and when he heard the story he went after Death and wrestled with him. Then a veiled woman appeared from the Underworld, who seemed to be Alkestis rescued by Herakles.

This story, as I read it, tells one of the profound, inexplicable mysteries of love. Love always has a close relation to death. I think of the death of Alkestis more like the death of Narcissus in his pool. Love takes us out of life and away from the plans we have made for our lives. Alkestis is an image of the feminine face of the soul whose destiny is to move out of life toward depth, which is imagined as death and underworld. Submission entails a loss in life, but there is also a gain for the soul. As the Greeks taught, the psyche is at home in the underworld. Love may seem to offer some benefits for the ego and for life, but soul is fed by love's intimacy with death. The loss of will and control one feels in love may be highly nutritious for the soul.

Still, the deathly side of love is not easy. It offends our upper-world values and expectations, and it contradicts the need to be in charge. We can all be like Admetus' parents when death appears, and find excellent excuses for declining the invitation. We can also become heroic and, like Herakles, wrestle what we want from the clutches of death. There may be an Alkestis in my heart willing to submit to the demands of love, but there may also be a Herakles who becomes furious at the idea and fights death with muscle.

Besides, the story is ambivalent and mysterious in its ending. Is this Alkestis returning from down below? Why does she have a veil over her face? Could it be that when we forcefully bring back to life what has been lost through love what we get is only a shade of its former reality? Maybe we can never succeed fully in restoring the soul to life. Maybe she will always be veiled and at least partially shielded from the rigors of actual life. Love demands a submission that is total.

In our therapeutic attempts to make life successful we act like Herakles, rescuing the soul from death. We save a person from depression by getting him involved in life in an active way—exactly what Herakles wants. But then we are faced with a veiled soul, someone who is adapted but also camouflaged, suffering distortion in his

soul. The alternative to this heroic struggle on behalf of life is to find something Alkestislike in us that is willing to go under, to *undergo* whatever fate is asking of the soul.

We think we know what love is about, both theoretically and in an episode in life. But love leans toward the mysterious dark niches of the soul's underworld. Its fulfillment is death—more an ending of what life has been up to this point than the beginning of what we expect to happen. Love takes us to the edge of what we know and have experienced, and thus we are all Alkestis whenever we assent to love and willingly accompany him in the guise of death.

Communal Love

One of the strongest needs of the soul is for community, but community from the soul point of view is a little different from its social forms. Soul yearns for attachment, for variety in personality, for intimacy and particularity. So it is these qualities in community that the soul seeks out, and not like-mindedness and uniformity.

There are many signs in our society that we lack a sufficiently deep experience of community. There is the energetic search for a community, as people try one church after another, hoping to have their unnamable hunger for community satisfied. They bemoan the breakdown of family and neighborhoods, longing for a past golden age when intimacy could be found at home or on the city block. Loneliness is a major complaint and is responsible for deep-seated emotional pain that leads to despair and a consideration of suicide.

The Renaissance humanist Erasmus says in his book *In Praise of Folly* that people are joined in friendship through their foolishness. Community cannot be sustained at too high a level. It thrives in the valleys of soul rather than in the heights of spirit.

Loneliness can be the result of an attitude that community is something into which one is received. Many people wait for members of a community to invite them

Bego with Company *by Niko Pirosmanashvili, 1907.*

in, and until that happens they are lonely. There may be something of the child here who expects to be taken care of by the family. But a community is not a family. It is a group of people held together by feelings of belonging, and those feelings are not a birthright. "Belonging" is an active verb, something we do positively. In one of his letters Ficino makes the remark "The one guardian of life is love, but to be loved you must love." A person oppressed by loneliness can go out into the world and simply start belonging to it, not by joining organizations, but by living through feelings of relatedness—to other people, to nature, to society, to the world as a whole. Relatedness is a signal of soul. By allowing the sometimes vulnerable feelings of relatedness, soul pours into life and doesn't have to insist on itself symptomatically.

Like all activities of the soul, community has its connection to death and the underworld. From the point of view of the soul, the dead are as much a part of community as the living. Jung makes a mysterious comment in the prologue to his memoirs: "Other people are established inalienably in my memories only if their names were entered in the scrolls of my destiny from the beginning, so that encountering them was at the same time a kind of recollection." Outward community flourishes when we are in touch with the inner persons who crowd our dreams and waking thoughts. To overcome loneliness, we might consider releasing these inner figures into life, like the one who wants to sing or cuss in anger or is more sensual or more critical or even more needy than "I" would like to admit. To "admit" who I am is to "admit" those people into life, so that the inner community serves as a start for a sense of belonging in life.

Love keeps the soul on the track of its fate and keeps consciousness at the edge of the abyss of the infinity that is the range of the soul. This doesn't mean that relationships between people are not important to the soul's loves. Quite the opposite: recognizing the importance of love to the soul, our ordinary human loves are ennobled beyond measure. This family, this friend, this lover, this mate is the manifestation of the motivating force of life itself and is the fountain of love that keeps the soul alive and full. There is no way toward divine love except through the discovery of human intimacy and community. One feeds the other.

Care of the soul, then, requires an openness to love's many forms. It is no accident that so many of the troubles we bring to therapy have their roots or manifestations in love. It may help us, in those times of trouble, to remember that love is not only about relationship, it is also an affair of the soul. Disappointments in love, even betrayals and losses, serve the soul at the very moment they seem in life to be tragedies. The soul is partly in time and partly in eternity. We might remember the part that resides in eternity when we feel despair over the part that is in life.

The Evocation of the Butterflies *by Odilon Redon, 1910–12.*

CHAPTER FIVE

Jealousy and Envy: Healing Poisons

EVEN THOUGH CARE OF THE SOUL is not about changing, fixing, adjusting, and making better, still we have to find a way to live with our disturbing feelings, such as jealousy and envy. These emotions can be so sickening and corrosive that we don't want to leave them raw, wallowing in them for years and getting nowhere with them. But what can we do short of trying to get rid of them? A clue is to be found in the very distaste we feel for them: anything so difficult to accept must have a special kind of shadow in it, a germ of creativity shrouded in a veil of repulsion. As we have so often found, in matters of the soul the most unworthy pieces turn out to be the most creative. The stone the builders reject becomes the cornerstone.

Both envy and jealousy are common experiences. Either emotion can make a person feel ugly. There is nothing noble in either of them. At the same time, a person may feel oddly attached to them.

Mythology suggests that both envy and jealousy are rooted deeply in the soul. Even the gods become jealous. Euripides' *Hippolytus*, for instance, is based

Jealousy by Edvard Munch, 1863–1944.

Above: Il Parnasso *by Andrea Mantegna, 1496. While Mars and Venus stand above the revellers Cupid informs Haephestus of his wife's infidelity.* Opposite: *Head of Venus, 5th c. BCE.*

on the myth of a young man who is exclusively devoted to the pure goddess, Artemis. Aphrodite is bitterly upset about his single-mindedness and his disdain for the part of life she tends, chiefly love and sex. Enraged and jealous, Aphrodite causes Hippolytus' stepmother, Phaedra, to fall in love with him. Naturally, all kinds of complications and mayhem ensue: in the end, Hippolytus is trampled to death by his horses, panicked by a giant, bull-shaped wave created in the sea by Aphrodite.

In Greek tragedy the gods and goddesses address us directly. At the opening of Euripides' play about Hippolytus, Aphrodite confesses, "I stir up trouble for any who ignore me, or belittle me, and who do it out of stub-born pride." Here we find a Freudian observation from the fifth century B.C.—repress sexuality and you are in for trouble.

Jealousy

I f the sacred arts of tragedy and mythology tell us that the gods are jealous, then we can imagine that there is a necessity to this emotion's fitting into the divine scheme of things. Jealousy is not simply insecurity or emotional instability. If the gods are jealous, then our experience of jealousy is archetypal, not completely explained by relationship or personality or family background. The tension we feel in jealousy may be that of much greater worlds colliding than can be seen by looking only at our personal situations.

The story of Hippolytus gives us a hint about the purpose of jealousy. Here was a man who routinely and consciously neglected a goddess whose task it is to foster an extremely important dimension of human life—love, sex, beauty, and the body. It's all right, the goddess declares, to be devoted to Artemistic purity and self-suffi-ciency, but desire for another is also valid and important. Aphrodite's jealous anger and the young man's undoing arise because he neglects her necessity. Hippolytus' offense is to deny the polytheistic requirements of the soul.

Thinking mythologically, we might imagine our own pain, paranoid suspicions, and jealous rages as the complaint of a god who is receiving insufficient attention. We may be like Hippolytus, sincerely and honestly devoted to principles that we consider absolute, while, unknown to us, other different, seemingly incompatible demands are also coming our way. Hippolytus' haughty purity and vitriolic hatred of women can be seen as his refusal to open himself to a world *other* than that which he has come to love and admire. In the end he is destroyed by the very animals who represent his self-sufficient spirit.

The Bath of Hera. *Ludovisi relief, 5th c.* BCE.

The name Hippolytus means "horse-loosed." A person caught in this myth is someone whose horses, animals of spirit, are not contained. They have leapt the fences of the corral. They are beautiful but dangerous. You sometimes see this Hippolytus horse-spirit in people, not always literally young, who are fervently devoted to a cult or cause. Their motives and the objects of their devotion are noble and spotless, and their commitment may be inspiring. But their very single-minded-ness may reveal something darker—a blindness to other values and sometimes even a sadistic element, a too readily justified show of muscle.

But jealousy, like all emotions tinted with shadow, can be a blessing in disguise, a poison that heals. Euripides' play can be seen as a story about curing Artemistic pride. Hippolytus, rigid and closed, is torn apart; that is, his spiritual neurosis is healed by becoming unraveled. The end appears tragic, but tragedy, even in everyday life, can be a form of valuable restructuring. It is painful and in some ways destructive, but it also puts things in a new order. The only way *out of* jealousy is *through* it. We may have to

let jealousy have its way with us and do its job of reorienting fundamental values. Its pain comes, at least in part, from opening up to unexplored territory and letting go of old familiar truths in the face of unknown and threatening new possibilities.

Hera: Goddess of Jealousy

Aphrodite and Artemis are not the only images of jealousy we find in mythology. All the gods and goddesses are capable of violent rages, but foremost in jealousy is Hera, wife of Zeus.

It's curious that in Greek mythology the wife of the greatest of the gods is known primarily for her jealousy. She isn't the queen who cares for the suffering of her subjects. She isn't absolute beauty fulfilling absolute power. She is a fitful, outrageously infuriated, betrayed, and violated wife. Hera's rage is as much the color of her jealousy as lust is the tone of Zeus's world governance. It is as though jealousy were as important to the maintenance of life and culture as Zeus's counsel and political power. Mythologically, jealousy is coupled with the forces of governance in life and culture.

Zeus, who settles the fundamental disputes of existence and serves as the original "god-father," lusts after every particular in the world he governs. While his desire goes out to the world, Hera's rage speaks for the home, for family and marriage. Erotic creativity is the making of a world, jealousy is the preservation of the hearth and interiority.

One of the stumbling blocks for a monotheist approaching a polytheistic religion is the validation one finds everywhere in polytheism of unlikely experiences. In the religion of Hera, one of the great virtues is possessiveness. From her point of view, it is not only all right, it is required that one be outraged at infidelity. In a culture that prizes individual freedom and choice, the desire to possess is a piece of shadow, but it is also a real desire. Jealousy is fulfilled in true connection with another person. But this connection makes severe demands. It asks us to love attachment and dependence, to risk the unbearable pain of separation, and to find fulfillment in partnership with another—a traditional attribute of Hera.

The Archetypal Wife

In Hera, a person is most an individual when he or she is defined in relation to another, even though this idea seems to go against all our modern notions of the value of independence and separateness. In our time it doesn't seem right to find identity in relationship to another. Yet this is the mystery of Hera. She is dependency given dignity and even divinity. In ancient times she was given great honor and was worshiped with deep affection and reverence. When people complain that whenever they get into a relationship they become too dependent, we might see this symptom as a lack of Hera sensibility, and the tonic might be to cultivate an appreciation for deeper union in love and attachment.

It takes special skill and sensitivity for a man or woman to evoke the wife within a relationship. Usually we reduce the archetypal reality to a social role. A woman slips into the role of wife, and the man treats her as being in that role. But there is a vast difference between archetype and role. There are ways that Hera can be drawn into the relationship so that being an attentive and serving partner is vitally present in both people. Or Hera might be evoked as the atmosphere of mutual dependency and identity as a couple. In the spirit of Hera, the couple protects the relationship and values signals of their dependency. For Hera, you make a phone call when you're on a trip or out of town. For Hera, you include your partner in visions of the future.

Feelings of jealousy may well be attached to this dependent element in the partnership. Jealousy is part of the archetype. Hera is loving and jealous. But when the value of true companionship is not taken to heart, Hera leaves the scene, and the rela-

Hera, *5th c.* BCE.

tionship is reduced to mere togetherness. Then the individuals split themselves into the independent one who stands for freedom and the "codependent" one, tormented by jealousy. If in a marriage one of the partners is clearly the wife—and it's not always the woman—then Hera is not being honored. If you are faced with symptoms of a troubled marriage, look for her distress.

The marriage that Hera honors so fervently is not only the concrete relationship of man and woman, it is any kind of connection, emotional or cosmic. As Jung says, marriage is always an affair of the soul. Hera may also protect the union of distinct elements within a person or in a society.

Karl Kerényi, the historian who was a friend of Jung and who developed his own archetypal approach to mythology, makes an intriguing comment in his book, *Zeus and Hera*. Hera was fulfilled, he tells us, in lovemaking. (That word *fulfilled*, by the way, is a special Hera word; other Greek words used as attributes of Hera are related to the word *telos*, which means end or purpose.) Kerényi is saying, then, that it is essential in Hera to find her purpose and fulfillment in sex. It may seem obvious that sex is part of being a wife, but I want to accent the idea that this particular side of sex, the fulfillment of intimacy and companionship, has its divinity. Hera was honored as Zeus's lover. The "Homeric Hymn to Hera" tells us that she and Zeus enjoyed a three-hundred-year honeymoon. Furthermore, Kerényi mentions that Hera renewed her virginity each year in the spring Kanathos, an actual spring where the cult statue fo Hera was dipped in an annual ritual, and so she presented herself to Zeus as a girl and was then fulfilled in her sexuality.

In Jungian language, we could say that Hera is part of the *anima* of sex. In the marriage bed, partners can encounter each other as if for the first time, thus enjoying this Hera imagination of renewable virginity. If a relationship honors Hera, it is blessed with the pleasures of experiencing the fulfillment of the sexual bond between

Above: Hera *from a vase, 5th c.* BCE. *Opposite:* Hera, *5th c.* BCE.

the people. The problem is, Hera cannot be evoked without her full nature, including her jealousy and her wifehood, which may at times be accompanied by feelings of inferiority and dependence. To find soul in relationship and in sex, it may be necessary to appreciate the inferior feelings that are part of the "wife" archetype.

The God who brings the disease, it is said, is the one who heals it. This is the "wounding healer" or the "healing wounder." If the disease is jealousy, then the healer could be Hera, who knows jealousy better than anyone. Therefore, we are back where we began. If we want to cure our jealousy, we may have to enter into it homeopathically. Those very qualities that are so pronounced in jealousy— dependency, identity through another, the longing to protect the union—may have to be taken even closer to heart so that Hera can be honored. If jealousy is compulsive and overwhelming, then maybe Hera is complaining of neglect and the fact that the relationship does not have the soulfulness that only she can bring to it. Strangely, perhaps jealousy itself contains the seeds of the fulfillment of both sex and intimacy.

Envy

Similar to jealousy in the way it jabs at the heart is envy, one of the seven deadly sins and clearly serious shadow material. Once again we ask a difficult question: How do you care for the soul when it is presenting itself in the green ooze of envy? Can we give this deadly sin an open-minded hearing? Can we perceive what the soul wants when it wrenches us with longing for what another person has?

Envy can be consuming. It can crowd out every other thought and emotion with its pungency. It can make a person distracted, "touched," as we say, aching for the life, position, and possessions of others.

Compulsions are always made up of two parts, and envy is no exception. On the one hand, envy is a desire for something, and on the other, it is a resistance to what the heart actually wants. In envy, desire and self-denial work together to create a characteristic sense of frustration and obsessiveness. Although envy feels masochistic—the envious person thinks he's the victim of bad fortune—it also involves strong willfulness in the form of resistance to fate and character.

The point in caring for the envious soul is not to get rid of the envy, but to be guided back by it into one's own fate. The pain in envy is like pain in the body: it makes us stop and take notice of something that has gone wrong and needs attention. What has gone wrong is that our close-up vision has been blurred. Envy is hyperopia of the soul, an inability to see what is closest to us. We fail to see the necessity and value in our own lives.

I once knew a woman who suffered for years from excruciating, exquisite, unrelenting envy. She worked hard all day at her factory job, trying to make her life better, and then she hid out at night in her house. She couldn't bear to behold what full lives people around her were living. She felt unconsolably lonely and utterly miserable. Over and over she described her friends' happiness in great detail. She knew everything good that happened to them. Whenever word came of some new success or boon to any of her friends, she went into shock, another nail pounded into the chest of envious thoughts she carried with her at all times.

The hidden side of masochism is willful tyranny. The misery of this woman's envy veiled her rigidity. Those very friends whom she envied she also judged without mercy. In her own family, she hovered over her two sons, who were in their thirties, and tried to control their every move. She appeared to be selfless in giving her whole life to their welfare and in depriving herself, but she also took pleasure in being in charge of someone else's life. Her envy mirrored her preoccupation with the lives of others and the neglect of her own.

The Dance of Life *by Edvard Munch. The three stages of a woman's life are depicted—the maiden, the nymph and the crone.*

Sidonia von Bork *by Edward Burne-Jones. Sidonia was a powerful sorceress who plotted the downfall and death of all those she envied.*

When she came to me for help with her envy, I thought I might invite it in and hear what it had to say. She, of course, claimed she wanted me to find a clever way out of it. But envy is like jealousy in that the person is actually attached to it and would like everyone else to be drawn into it. A person talking about envy is like a religious missionary trying to win converts. Behind the stories of envy is the message: Aren't you as outraged as I am? But, I didn't want to get caught in her sense of outrage. I wanted to know what the envy was doing there and what it had in mind.

We began our work by slowly going through her many, many stories of deprivation. I watched for ways in which she subtly distanced herself from pain and awareness. For example, she would make excuses for her family. "They didn't know any better. They did their best. Their intentions were good." I tried to go beyond these rationalizations so we could both feel the sadness and emptiness that had been in her past and to acknowledge the limitations and failures on the part of her parents. If in envy the person wishes life were better, then maybe it's a good idea to feel that emptiness deeply. It was fairly clear that what this woman was lacking was the capacity to feel her own sense of desolation and emptiness.

Once she began to speak more honestly about her home life and more realistically about her friends, who experienced as much misfortune as anyone might, the whining tone of envy in her voice gave way to something more solid and sober. She could then take more responsibility for her situation, and over time eventually improve it.

The fact that jealousy and envy are both resistant to reason and to human efforts to eradicate them is a blessing. They ask us for a deeper diving into the soul, beyond ideas of health and happiness and into mystery. It is the gods who become jealous and envious, and only by touching that deep place of divine activity can the individual make a response that is transforming, that takes him to an unfamiliar place where the mythical impulse stirs. Ultimately, these troublesome emotions offer a path to a life experienced with greater depth, maturity, and flexibility.

Our task is to care for the soul, but it is also true that the soul cares for us. So the phrase "care of the soul" can be heard in two ways. In one sense, we do our best to honor whatever the soul presents to us; in the other, the soul is the subject who does the caring. Even in its pathology, and maybe especially then, the soul cares for us by offering a way out of a narrow secularism. Its suffering can only be relieved by the reestablishment of a particular mythical sensibility. Therefore, its suffering initiates a move toward increased spirituality. Ironically, pathology can be a route to soulful religion.

CHAPTER SIX

The Soul and Power

IN THE SOUL, POWER DOESN'T WORK the same way as it does in the ego and will. When we want to accomplish something egoistically, we gather our strength, develop a strategy, and apply every effort. This is the kind of behavior James Hillman describes as heroic or Herculean. He means the word in the bad sense: using brute strength and narrow, rationalistic vision. The power of the soul, in contrast, is more like a great reservoir or, in traditional imagery, like the force of water in a fast-rushing river. It is natural, not manipulated, and stems from an unknown source. Our role with this kind of power is to be an attentive observer noticing how the soul wants to thrust itself into life. It is also our task to find artful means of articulating and structuring that power, taking full responsibility for it, but trusting too that the soul has intentions and necessities that we may understand only partially.

I am reminded here of Jung's constant attempt in both his theory and in his own life to discover the "transcendent function," as he called it, a point of view that embraces the mysterious depths of the soul as well as conscious understanding and intention. This, for Jung, was exactly what *self* means: it is a fulcrum of action and intelligence that feels the weight both of the soul and

East Twelfth Street *by Ben Shahn, 1946.*

of the intellect. This is not a mere theoretical construct. It can be, as Jung showed in his own soul work, a way of life.

What is the source of this soul power, and how can we tap into it? I believe it often comes from unexpected places. It comes first of all from living close to the heart, and not at odds with it. Therefore, paradoxically, soul power may emerge from failure, depression, and loss. The general rule is that soul appears in the gaps and holes of experience. It is usually tempting to find some subtle way of denying these holes or distancing ourselves from them. But we have all experienced moments when we've lost a job or endured an illness only to find an unexpected inner strength.

Writers are taught to "write what you know about." The same advice applies to the quest for the power of the soul: be good at what you're good at. Many of us spend time and energy trying to be something that we are not. But this is a move against soul, because individuality rises out of the soul as water rises out of the depths of the earth. We are who we are because of the special mix that makes up our soul. In spite of its archetypal, universal contents, for each individual the soul is highly idiosyncratic. Power begins in knowing this special soul, which may be entirely different from our fantasies about who we are or who we want to be.

A friend once introduced me to an audience I was about to lecture. "I'm going to tell you," he said to the group, "what Tom isn't. He isn't an artist, he isn't a scholar, he isn't a philosopher, he isn't . . ." I felt somewhat mortified hearing all these things I wasn't. At the time I was teaching at a university and was supposed to give the illusion at least that I was a scholar. Yet I knew I wasn't. My friend's unusual introduction was wise and absolutely correct. Maybe we could all use an emptying out of identity now and then. Considering who we are not, we may find the surprising revelation of who we are. Again, the *Tao Te Ching* (ch. 22), that absolute testament of soulful emptiness, says in words that also echo sayings of Jesus, "When twisted, you'll be upright; when hollowed out, you'll be full."

Soulful emptiness is not anxious. In fact, power pours in when we sustain the feeling of emptiness and withstand temptations to fill it prematurely. We have to contain the void. Too often we lose this pregnant emptiness by reaching for substitutes for power. A tolerance of weakness, you might say, is a prerequisite for the discovery of power, for any exercise of strength motivated by an avoidance of weakness is not genuine power. This is a rule of thumb. The soul has no room in which to present itself if we continually fill all the gaps with bogus activities.

The Logic and Language of the Soul

One of the central difficulties involved in embarking on care of the soul is grasping the nature of the soul's discourse. The intellect works with reasons, logic, analysis, research, equations, and pros and cons. But the soul practices a different kind of math and logic. It presents images that are not immediately intelligible to the reasoning mind. It insinuates, offers fleeting impressions, persuades more with desire than with reasonableness. In order to tap the soul's power, one has to be conversant with its style, and watchful.

Two Sufi stories demonstrate how odd the logic of the soul can appear to the reasoning, heroic mind. In the first, Nasrudin goes to a teacher for music lessons.

"How much do the lessons cost?" he asks.

"Fifteen dollars for the first lesson, ten dollars each after that," says the teacher.

"Fine," Nasrudin replies, "I'll begin with lesson number two."

I don't know if there is a canonical reading of this story, but to me it describes the mercurial wit of the soul from which a great deal of power can arise, as well as the special logic which goes against natural expectations. The alchemists taught that soul work is an *opus contra naturam*, a work against nature. This story is an example of how the soul's understanding of things is "unnatural."

The other Sufi story is more mysterious.

Nuri Bey was a reflective and respected Albanian who married a wife much younger than himself.

One evening when he had returned home earlier than usual, a faithful servant came to him and said, "Your wife, our mistress, is acting suspiciously. She is in her apartments with a huge chest, large enough to hold a man, which belonged to your

Right: Koum Kapi prayer rug *in silk and metal-thread.*

grandmother. It should contain only a few ancient embroideries. I believe that there may now be much more in it. She will not allow me, your oldest retainer, to look inside."

Nuri went to his wife's room and found her sitting disconsolately beside the massive wooden box.

"Will you show me what is in the chest?" he asked.

"Because of the suspicion of a servant, or because you do not trust me?"

"Would it not be easier just to open it, without thinking about the undertones?" asked Nuri.

"I do not think it possible."

"Is it locked?"

"Yes."

"Where is the key?"

She held it up. "Dismiss the servant and I will give it to you."

The servant was dismissed. The woman handed over the key and herself withdrew, obviously troubled in mind.

Nuri Bey thought for a long time. Then he called four gardeners from his estate. Together they carried the chest by night unopened to a distant part of the grounds, and buried it.

The matter was never referred to again.

This is a captivating and mysterious story. Again, I don't know if there is a canonical reading. To me it shows the soul, typically represented by the woman, as the vessel of mystery. The older man, the *senex*, wants to open this vessel and have the mystery explained. There is some shadow in the story, the suggestion that there could be a man in this chest. Or is it that whatever vessel the wife has can hold humanity or a person, as though it were the envelope of the human soul? The wife, again speaking for the soul, inquires into the fantasies of her husband about the chest. But, in typical Hercules fashion, he wants to dismiss the "undertone" and go directly to a literal solution: just open the box. From the wife's point of view it's simply not possible just to open the chest without taking the undertones into consideration.

But she has the key. Jung says that the *anima* is the face of the soul. In this story she is the one who can open and close the container. The tension centers around whether or not the man will force an opening of the box. Do we need to expose everything that is hidden? Do we need to understand all mysteries?

This is a teaching story, because we are taught in the end how to deal with the stuff of the soul. Nuri Bey thinks for a long time. He creates his own inner space with his reflection, and then he is ready for the kind of action that is appropriate for the soul. From the point of view of soul it is just as important, maybe more important, to check the urgency of curiosity and suspicion, to allow certain things to remain distant and buried, to trust one's soul mate or mate soul with things that shouldn't be brought to the light of day.

A man told me once about the woman he was in love with. They had had a quarrel and he had sent a rash, thoughtless letter to her in the heat of his distress. Before the letter arrived by mail, he telephoned her and asked her not to read the letter. She told him later that the letter had arrived and she had torn it up immediately. She had felt enormous curiosity, and on the torn, crinkled paper lying in the waste basket she could see the scribbles of his writing. She confessed she was tempted, but she let it go unread. At that moment, the man told me, he felt they had an unbroken bond between them. Their relationship had been tightened by her reverence. When he told me the story, I thought of Nuri Bey, and the special lesson in the power of soul he learned in his moments of thought when it was decided for him that the chest would remain closed.

Those stories showed that power is not always revealed in action. Nuri Bey could easily have overpowered his wife and discovered her secrets, but by preserving her privacy he maintains his power. In general, we keep our power when we protect the power of others.

Violence and the Need for Power

The word *violence* comes from the Latin word *vis*, meaning "life force." Its very roots suggest that in violence the thrust of life is making itself visible. If that fundamental vitality is not present in the heart, it nevertheless seems to appear distorted by our repressions and compromises, our fears and our narcissistic manipulations.

It would be a mistake to approach violence with any simple idea of getting rid of it. Chances are, if we try to eradicate our violence, we will also cut ourselves off from the deep power that sustains creative life. Besides, psychoanalysis teaches, repression never accomplishes what we want. The repressed always returns in monstrous form. The life current of the soul, *vis*, is like the natural force of plant life, like the grass that grows up through cement and in a relatively short time obliterates grand monuments of culture. If we try taming and boxing in this innate power, it will inevitably find its way into the light.

"Repression of the life force" is a diagnosis I believe would fit most of the emotional problems people present in therapy. Renaissance doctors placed both anger and the life force under the aegis of one god, Mars. All people, they taught, have an explosive force ready within them to be unleashed into the world. Simply being oneself—letting one's individuality and unique gifts come forth—is a manifestation of Mars. When we allow ourselves to exist truly and fully, we *sting* the world with our vision and challenge it with our own ways of being.

But throughout human history the expression of individuality has been felt as a threat to the status quo. For all its expressed championing of the individual, our cul-

Trouble *by Ben Shahn, 1947.*

ture in many ways favors conformity. We are pleasantly sedated by the flatness and predictability of modern life. You can travel far and wide and have a difficult time finding a store or restaurant that is even mildly unique. In shopping malls everywhere, in restaurant districts, in movie theaters, you will find the same clothes, the same brand names, the same menus, the same few films, the identical architecture. Yet, as psychoanalysis says, repetition is death. Repetition defends against the rush of individual life. It seeks the deadly peace of a culture that has banished surprise.

It is not unusual for repressed forces and symptoms eventually to reappear as objects; that is, our fantasy becomes crystallized in a thing that has the power and lure of a fetish. In this sense our nuclear arsenals with their mystery and threat are dark carriers of what has been ignored in the soul. Bombs and missiles give us a constant, daily association with our own destruction. They are reminders that every-

thing cannot be contained and controlled, that as a society we can kill ourselves and obliterate other peoples and the planet itself. This is an unprecedented fetish of power. Because we have refused to associate ourselves with the darker forces, they have been forced into fetishistic form, where they remain, fascinating and lethal.

I see a connection, therefore, between our seemingly insoluble violence and our treasured repetitious flatness. The soul, tradition has taught us for centuries, needs the profound and challenging grace of Mars, who reddens everything in his vicinity with the glow of passionate life, brings a creative edge to every action, and sows the seeds of power in every moment and event. When Mars is overlooked and undervalued, he is forced to appear in fetish and in violent behavior. Mars is infinitely greater than personal expression of anger. Creative and destructive, he is life itself poised for struggle.

There is nothing neutral about the soul. It is the seat and the source of life. Either we respond to what the soul presents in its fantasies and desires, or we suffer from this neglect of ourselves.

Sadomasochism

When the soul's power is neglected, usurped, or toyed with, then we fall into the truly problematical condition of sadomasochism, which can range from being an extreme clinical syndrome to a dynamic at work in the most ordinary, simple transactions. Genuine power,

The Body of Abel found by Adam and Eve *by William Blake, 1826.*

in which there are no tyrants and no literal victims, breaks, in sadomasochism, into two parts: violence and victimization, controller and subject. Sadomasochism, though it may look superficially like genuine strength, is a failure of power. Whenever one person victimizes another, real power has been lost and replaced by a literalistic drama that is dangerous for both parties.

The sadomasochistic splitting of power has the characteristics of all symptomatic behavior: it is literally destructive, and it involves a polarization in which one side of the split is apparent, while the other is hidden. People who turn to violence are visibly controlling; what is less obvious are their weakness and feelings of powerlessness. On the other hand, those who habitually play the victim may be quite unaware of their own more subtle methods of control. This is why issues of power are so difficult to deal with: things are not as they appear to be.

The Dark Angel of Destruction

Violence has a great deal to do with shadow, in particular the shadow of power. For many people born and raised in modern America, innocence—the absence or rejection of shadow—is a strong obstacle to realizing the soul's power. When people talk about power and innocence, they often refer to their religious upbringing, which in one way or another taught them to turn the other cheek and to suffer. David Miller has pointed out that the image of churchgoers as a flock of sheep in a subtle way maintains the notion that to be good is to be weak and submissive.

Discord *by Ben Shahn, 1953.*

Another way power is lost is by identifying with the *puer* fantasy that is so strong in the American psyche. The youthful spirit of idealism, the melting pot, everyone has a chance, all people are equal—these tenets of the American ideal not only cast a dark shadow, they also make power seem undesirable to many people. It gets repressed as shadow material, and as a result many power struggles take place in secret, in an underhanded way.

Dreams frequently present images of dark power in which the dreamer is either the wielder of weapons or their victim. For example, a middle-aged man told me this dream: He was standing outside the door of a bank, waiting for it to be opened. A woman was standing with him, along with a few other people. Suddenly he noticed that two men near him had guns in their pockets. He could see the tips of the handles sticking out, and he saw that the men were slowly sliding them out to go into action. Instinctively he began to run away in panic at the thought of gunshots. He left his friend in the dust, without a care for her, and he woke up feeling guilty about his cowardice.

The man understood his dream as a portrait of his fear of violence. He had great difficulty in the most ordinary confrontations. It would be characteristic of him, he told me, to be overly solicitous about his companion, but in the dream panic over-shadowed his altruism, and he made an amazingly speedy retreat.

I saw the two men as dark angels, doing something the dreamer would never think of doing. He was frightened by their guns and ran from them, but maybe he wasn't being cowardly. Flight seems like a sensible response in the presence of guns, especially when you yourself don't have one. We could also see his move away from the woman as something that happens when he senses violence. He is no longer close to the feminine, sensitive world he habitually thinks he should protect.

The dream wasn't just about guns, it also involved robbing a bank. The dream could be seen as a lesson in the necessity of thievery. Sometimes you have to put on a dark mask, carry a weapon in your pocket—in the phallic region and in the female pouch—in order to get along.

Religion is filled with puzzling tales of amoral financial arrangements. Jesus tells the story of the manager who paid the same wages to people who worked for an hour as to those who worked an entire day. The Greeks celebrated the tale of Hermes, who on the first day of his life stole the cattle of his brother Apollo. In order to enjoy the gifts of Hermes, it may be necessary to have our Apollonic values robbed. The story of Nasrudin and the music lesson sounds like an invitation to cheat. In the Gospel story and in countless paintings of the crucifixion, Jesus is shown on a cross between two thieves, one of whom he says will be in heaven with him. This image is sometimes interpreted as the humiliation of Jesus, but the story may also be an elevation of thieving.

Oscar Wilde's letter from prison known as "De Profundis," "from the depths," is an extraordinary example of Romantic theology, and in it he discusses the place of shadow in the image of Jesus:

The world had always loved the saint as being the nearest possible approach to the perfection of God. Christ, through some divine instinct in him, seems to have always loved the sinner as being the nearest possible approach to the perfection of man. His primary desire was not to reform people any more than his desire was to relieve suffering. . . . But in a manner not yet understood of the world he regarded sin and suffering as being in themselves beautiful holy things and modes of perfection.

Anyone who talks glibly about integrating the shadow, as if you could chum up to shadow the way you learn a foreign language, doesn't know the darkness that always qualifies shadow. Fear is never far removed from power. And genuine innocence is always to be found in the vicinity of blood-guilt. The three crosses on Golgotha do not simply represent the triumph of virtue over vice. They are a reflection of Christianity's most treasured image, the trinity. They hint at the great mystery Oscar Wilde points to: the fact that virtue is never genuine when it sets itself apart from evil. We only sustain violence in our world if we fail to admit its place in our own hearts and identify only with unaffecting innocence.

People frequently tell me dreams of guns and other kinds of weapons. I don't think this is a compensation for innocence in life as much as it is a sign that the soul loves power. Dreams give us a less censored view of the potential of the soul than a person's conscious self-analysis. There are signs in society, too, that the gun is a rit-

Oscar Wilde, *1854–1900*.

ual object. Guns are both banned and adored. A gun is one of the most numinous—mysteriously fascinating and disturbing—objects around us. Those who protest its banishment may be speaking for a rare idol of power that keeps the strength of life, *vis*, before our eyes. A gun is dangerous not only because it threatens our lives, but also because it concretizes and fetishizes our desire for power, keeping power both in sight and also removed from its soulful presence in our daily lives. The presence

Christest between the two thieves *by Rembrandt van Rijn.*

of the gun in our society is a threat, and we are its victims—a sign that our fetish is working against us.

It is often said that the gun is a phallic symbol. It is more likely the other way around: the phallus is a gun symbol. We are fascinated by the power of a gun, and it's interesting to note that the word fascinating originally referred to the phallus.

The soul is explosive and powerful. Through its medium of imagination, which is always a prerequisite for action and is the source of meaning, it can accomplish all things. In the strength of its emotions, the soul is a gun, full of potential power and effect. The pen, expressing the soul's passion, is mightier than the sword because the imagination can change the life of a people at their very roots.

If violence is the repressed life force showing itself symptomatically, then the cure for violence is care of the soul's power. It is foolish to deny signs of this power—individuality, eccentricity, self-expression, passion—because it cannot be truly repressed. If there is crime in our streets, it is due, from the viewpoint of soul, not just to poverty and difficult living conditions, but to the failure of the soul and its spirit to unveil themselves.

Socrates and Jesus, two teachers of virtue and love, were executed because of the unsettling, threatening power of their souls, which was revealed in their personal lives and in their words. They did not carry guns, yet still they were a threat, because there is nothing more powerful than the revelation of one's own soul. Here is another reason for placing Jesus between two thieves. He *was* a criminal in the eyes of a soul-denying authority. Criminality and transgression, when not acted out in violence, are dark virtues of the heart, necessary for the full presence of an individual on earth. Only when they are repressed do we find them roaming the streets of a city as incarnations of the rejected shadow.

A soulful life is never without shadow, and some of the soul's power comes from its shadow qualities. If we want to live from our depths—soulfully—then we will have to give up all pretenses to innocence as the shadow grows darker. The chief reward of surrendering innocence, so that the soul may be fully expressed, is an increase of power. In the presence of deep power, life becomes robust and passionate, signs that the soul is engaged and being given expression. Mars, when he is honored, gives a deep red hue to everything we do, quickening our lives with intensity, passion, forcefulness, and courage. When he is neglected, we suffer the onslaughts of uncontained violence. It is important, then, to revere the Marsian spirit and to let the soul burst into life—in creativity, individuality, iconoclasm, and imagination.

CHAPTER SEVEN

Gifts of Depression

THE SOUL PRESENTS ITSELF IN A VARIETY OF COLORS, including all the shades of gray, blue, and black. To care for the soul, we must observe the full range of all its colorings, and resist the temptation to approve only of white, red, and orange—the brilliant colors. The "bright" idea of colorizing old black and white movies is consistent with our culture's general rejection of the dark and the gray. In a society that is defended against the tragic sense of life, depression will appear as an enemy, an unredeemable malady; yet in such a society, devoted to light, depression, in compensation, will be unusually strong.

Care of the soul requires our appreciation of these ways it presents itself. Faced with depression, we might ask ourselves, "What is it doing here? Does it have some necessary role to play?" Especially in dealing with depression, a mood close to our feelings of mortality, we must guard against the denial of death that is so easy to slip into. Even further, we may have to develop a taste for the depressed mood, a positive respect for its place in the soul's cycles.

Some feelings and thoughts seem to emerge only in a dark mood. Suppress the mood, and you will suppress those ideas and reflections. Depression may be as

Melancholia, *engraving by Albrecht Durer.*

important a channel for valuable "negative" feelings as expressions of affection are for the emotions of love. Feelings of love give birth naturally to gestures of attachment. In the same way, the void and grayness of depression evoke an awareness and articulation of thoughts otherwise hidden behind the screen of lighter moods. Melancholy gives the soul an opportunity to express a side of its nature that is as valid as any other, but is hidden out of our distaste for its darkness and bitterness.

Left: Saturn *from an 18th century astrological treatise.* Opposite: *The Triumph of Time by Philip Galle, 1574.*

Saturn's Child

Today we seem to prefer the word *depression* over *sadness* and *melancholy*. Perhaps its Latin form sounds more clinical and serious. But there was a time, five or six hundred years ago, when melancholy was identified with the Roman god Saturn. To be depressed was to be "in Saturn," and a person chronically disposed to melancholy was known as a "child of Saturn." Since depression was identified with the God and

the planet named for him, it was associated with other qualities of Saturn. For example, he was known as the "old man," who presided over the golden age. Whenever we talk about the "golden years" or the "good old days," we are calling up this god, who is the patron of the past. The depressed person sometimes thinks that the good times are all past, that there is nothing left for the present or the future. These melancholic thoughts are deeply rooted in Saturn's preference for days gone by, for memory and the sense that time is passing. These thoughts and feelings, sad as they are, favor the soul's desire to be both in time and in eternity, and so in a strange way they can be pleasing.

Depression grants the gift of experience not as a literal fact but as an attitude toward yourself. You get a sense of having lived through something, of being older and wiser. You know that life is suffering, and that knowledge makes a difference. You can't enjoy the bouncy, carefree innocence of youth any longer, a realization

that entails both sadness because of the loss and pleasure in a new feeling of self-acceptance and self-knowledge. This awareness of age has a halo of melancholy around it, but it also enjoys a measure of nobility.

Naturally, there is resistance to this incursion of Saturn that we call depression. It's difficult to let go of youth, because that release requires an acknowledgment of death. I suspect that those of us who opt for eternal youth are setting ourselves up for heavy bouts of depression. We're inviting Saturn to make a house call when we try to delay our service to him. Then Saturn's depression will give its color, depth, and substance to the soul that for one reason or another has dallied long with youth. Saturn weathers and ages a person naturally, the way temperature, winds, and time weather a barn. In Saturn, reflection deepens, thoughts embrace a larger sense of time, and the events of a long lifetime get distilled into a sense of one's essential nature.

Aging brings out the flavors of a personality. The individual emerges over time, the way fruit matures and ripens. In the Renaissance view, depression, aging, and individuality all go together: the sadness of growing old is part of becoming an individual. Melancholy thoughts carve out an interior space where wisdom can take up residence.

Saturn was also traditionally identified with the metal lead, giving the soul weight and density, allowing the light, airy elements to coalesce. In this sense, depression is a process that fosters a valuable coagulation of thoughts and emotions. As we age, our ideas, formerly light, rambling, and unrelated to each other, become more densely gathered into values and a philosophy, giving our lives substance and firmness.

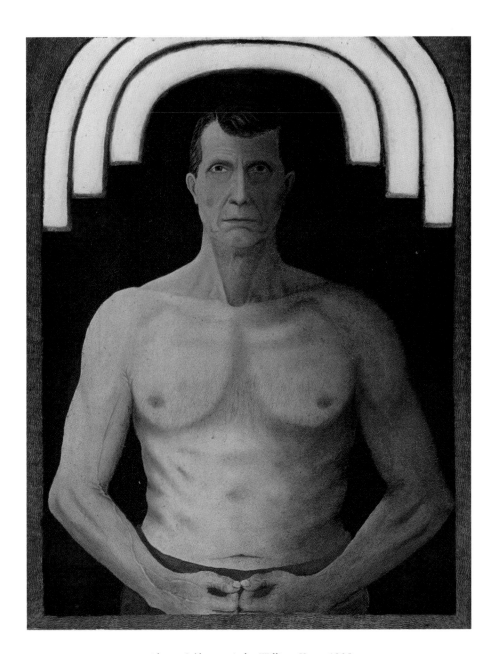

Above: Self-portrait *by William Kane, 1905.*

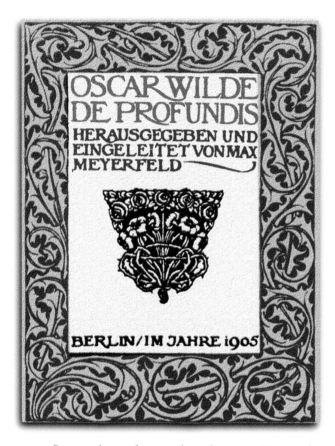

De Profundis *by Oscar Wilde was first published in Germany in 1905.*

Because of its painful emptiness, it is often tempting to look for a way out of depression. But entering into its mood and thoughts can be deeply satisfying. Depression is sometimes described as a condition in which there are no ideas—nothing to hang on to. But maybe we have to broaden our vision and see that feelings of emptiness, the loss of familiar understandings and structures in life, and the vanishing of enthusiasm, even though they seem negative, are elements that can be appropriated and used to give life fresh imagination.

Insinuations of Death

Saturn is also the reaper, god of the harvest, patron of end-time and its festival, the Saturnalia; accordingly, imagery of death may permeate periods of depression. People of all ages sometimes say from their depression that life is over, that their hopes for the future have proved unfounded. They are disillusioned because the values and understandings by which they have lived for years suddenly make no sense. Cherished truths sink into Saturn's black earth like chaff at harvest time.

The emptiness and dissolution of meaning that are often present in depression show how attached we can become to our ways of understanding and explaining our lives. Often our personal philosophies and our values seem to be all too neatly wrapped, leaving little room for mystery. Depression comes along then and opens up a hole.

This saturnine truth is evoked by Oscar Wilde, who, for all his emphasis on fullness of style as a central concern of life, knew the importance of emptying. The final mystery is oneself. When one has weighed the sun in the balance, and measured the steps of the moon, and mapped out the seven heavens star by star, there still remains oneself. Who can calculate the orbit of his own soul?

Coming to Terms with Depression

In Jungian language, Saturn may be considered an *animus* figure. The *animus* is a deep part of the psyche that roots ideas and abstraction in the soul. Many people are strong in *anima*—full of imagination, close to life, empathic, and connected to people around them. But these very people may have difficulty moving far enough away from emotional involvement to see what is going on, and to relate their life experiences to their ideas and values. Their experience is "wet," to use another ancient metaphor for the soul, because they are so emotionally involved in life, and so they might benefit from an excursion to the far-off regions of cold, dry Saturn.

This dryness can separate awareness from the moist emotions that are characteristic of close involvement with life. We see this development in old people as they reflect on

their past with some distance and detachment. In Samuel Beckett's melancholy play *Krapp's Last Tape,* we find a humorous, biting depiction of saturnine reflection. Using a tape recorder, Krapp plays back tapes he has made throughout his life, and listens with considerable gloom to his voices from the past. After one of the tapes, he sits down to make another: "Just listening to that stupid bastard I took myself for thirty years ago, hard to believe I was ever as bad as that. Thank God that's all done with anyway."

Krapp, whose name suggests depression's devaluation of human life, shows that cold remorse and self-judgment do not have to be seen as clinical syndromes, but as a necessary foolishness in human life that actually accomplishes something for the soul. Professional psychology might try to correct Krapp's self-criticism as a form of neurotic masochism, but Beckett shows that even in its ugliness and foolishness it makes a certain kind of sense.

The Race Track *by Albert Pinkham Ryder.*

Krapp playing his tapes and muttering his curses is also an image of ourselves turning our memories over in our minds again and again, in a process of distillation. Over time something essential emerges from this saturnine reduction—the gold in the sludge. Saturn was sometimes called *sol niger*, the black sun. In his darkness there is to be found a precious brilliance, our essential nature, distilled by depression as perhaps the greatest gift of melancholy.

If we persist in our modern way of treating depression as an illness to be cured only mechanically and chemically, we may lose the gifts of soul that only depression can provide. In particular, tradition taught that Saturn fixes, darkens, weights, and hardens whatever is in contact with it. If we do away with Saturn's moods, we may find it exhausting trying to keep life bright and warm at all costs. We may be even more overcome then by the increased melancholy called forth by the repression of Saturn, and lose the sharpness and substance of identity that Saturn gives the soul. Saturn locates identity deeply in the soul, rather than on the surface of personality. Identity is felt as one's soul finding its weight and measure. We know who we are because we have uncovered the stuff of which we are made. It has been sifted out by depressive thought, "reduced," in the chemical sense, to essence.

Care of the soul asks for a cultivation of the larger world depression represents. When we speak clinically of depression, we think of an emotional or behavioral condition, but when we imagine depression as a visitation by Saturn, then many qualities of his world come into view: the need for isolation, the coagulation of fantasy, the distilling of memory, and accommodation with death, to name only a few.

For the soul, depression is an initiation, a rite of passage. If we think that depression, so empty and dull, is void of imagination, we may overlook its initiatory aspects. We may be imagining imagination itself from a point of view foreign to Saturn; emptiness can be rife with feeling-tone, images of catharsis, and emotions of regret and loss. As a shade of mood, gray can be as interesting and as variegated as it is in black-and-white photography.

Saturn as the God of depression vomiting the Stone of Regeneration
from an 18th c. alchemical treatise.

If we pathologize depression, treating it as a syndrome in need of cure, then the emotions of Saturn have no place to go except into abnormal behavior and acting out. An alternative would be to invite Saturn in, when he comes knocking, and give him an appropriate place to stay. Some Renaissance gardens had a bower dedicated

to Saturn—a dark, shaded, remote place where a person could retire and enter the persona of depression without fear of being disturbed. We could model our attitude and our ways of dealing with depression on this garden. Sometimes people need to withdraw and show their coldness. As friends and counselors, we could provide the emotional space for such feelings, without trying to change them or interpret them. And as a society, we could acknowledge Saturn in our buildings. A house or commercial building could have a room or an actual garden where a person could go to withdraw in order to meditate, think, or just be alone and sit. Why is it that we fail to appreciate this facet of the soul? One reason is that most of what we know about Saturn comes to us symptomatically. Emptiness appears too late and too literally to have soul in it. In our cities, boarded-up homes and failing businesses signal economic and social "depression." In these "depressed" areas of our cities, decay is cut off from will and conscious participation, appearing only as an external manifestation of a problem or an illness.

Because depression is one of the faces of the soul, acknowledging it and bringing it into our relationships fosters intimacy. If we deny or cover up anything that is at home in the soul, then we cannot be fully present to others. Hiding the dark places results in a loss of soul; speaking for them and from them offers a way toward genuine community and intimacy.

The Healing Powers of Depression

A few years ago, Bill, a priest, came to me with a remarkable story. In his sixty-fifth year, thirty years into the priesthood, as a compassionate pastor of a rural church he had given what he thought was perfectly appropriate aid to two of his women parishioners. His bishop, however, thought he had mishandled church funds and used poor judgment in other respects, and so, after a lifetime of respect, he was given two days to pack and leave the diocese.

Left: Figure in a Landscape *by Premgit.*

Daphne *by Joan Hanley.*

When he began talking to me about his situation, Bill was quite lively and interested in his experiences. He had taken to group therapy well, where in particular he had found ways to engage some of his anger. He even decided at one point to become a therapist himself, with the idea that he might be able to help his fellow priests. But when he talked about the trouble he had fallen into, he gave me explanations and excuses that seemed naive.

As the naive explanations for his behavior fell away to be replaced by more substantive thoughts about the larger themes in his life, the tone of his mood darkened.

As he expressed more of his anger about the way he had been treated throughout his life as a seminarian and priest, he lost much of his lightness. Meanwhile, he had moved into a home for priests, where he was largely withdrawn. He embraced his solitude and decided not to participate in activities in the home, and gradually, the wounds of his recent experiences deepened into genuine depression.

Now, Bill spoke critically of the church authorities and talked more realistically about his father, who had tried to become a priest and had failed. To some extent Bill thought that he was not cut out by nature to be a priest, that he had taken his father's place, trying to fulfill his father's dreams and not his own.

Bill trusted his depression enough to allow it a central place in his life. But he remained in therapy, and every week he spoke from and about his depression.

My therapeutic strategy, if you can call it that, was simply to bring an attitude of acceptance and interest to Bill's depression. I simply tried to appreciate the way his soul was expressing itself at the moment.

In his depression, when Bill said that he should never have been a priest, I didn't take that statement literally, because I knew how much his priesthood had meant to Bill over the years. But now he was discovering the shadow in his calling. His life as a priest was being deepened, given soul, by new reflection on its limitations. Bill was having to face for the first time the sacrifices he had made in order to be a priest. This was not an absolute disavowal of his priesthood; it was a completion. I noticed that even as he uncovered piece after piece of the sacrifices he had made, and even as he felt intense regret for having become a priest, at the same time he spoke of his loyalty to the church, his continuing interest in theology, and his concern for death and afterlife. In some ways, he was only now discovering the real core of his priesthood. The docile, compulsively helpful priest was dying off, to be replaced by a stronger, more individual, less manipulated man.

One day he told me a dream in which he was going down a steep flight of stairs, then down a second flight; but the latter were too narrow for him and he didn't want to go any farther. Behind him the figure of a woman was urging him on, while he resisted. This was a picture of Bill's state at the time. He was well into a descent, but he was fighting against taking a deeper plunge.

Bill's complaint "I'm an old man; there's nothing left for me" was not really Saturn settling in. Although his statement sounds like an affirmation of age, it is more an attack on age. When he said this I wondered if he had been denied the opportunity to grow up during his many years as a seminarian and priest. He told me that in some ways he had felt like a child the whole time, never worrying about money or survival, never making life decisions, but simply following the orders of his superiors. Now fate had shoved him into a place of profound unsettling and reflection. For the first time he was questioning everything, and now he was growing up at an alarming speed.

"Your dream," I said to him, "about descending a narrow staircase with a woman urging you from behind—I think we might turn to Freud and see it as an attempt at birth."

"I never thought of it that way," he said, interested.

"You seem in your melancholy to be in a bardo state. Do you know what that is?"

"No," he said, "I never heard of it."

"The *Tibetan Book of the Dead* describes that time between incarnations, the period before the next birth into life, as bardo."

"I don't have any taste for the events of life these days."

"That's what I mean," I said. "You don't want to participate in life. You are between lives. The dream may be inviting you to descend into the canal."

"I feel very reluctant in that dream, and I'm disturbed by the woman."

"Aren't we all," I said, thinking how difficult it is to be born into this life again, especially when the first time around was so painful and apparently unsuccessful.

"I'm not ready," he said with understanding and conviction.

"That's all right," I responded. "You know where you are, and it's important to be exactly there. Bardo takes time; it can't be rushed. There's no point in premature birth."

Eventually Bill's depression lifted, and he took a position in a new city where he worked as both counselor and priest. His period of schooling in Saturn's truths had some effect. He was able to help people look honestly at their lives and their emotions, whereas at a former time he would have tried to talk them out of their dark

Saturn Watering the Sun and Moon Flowers in the Garden of Love, *from an 18th c. alchemical treatise.*

feelings with purely positive encouragement. He also knew what it was like to be deprived of respect and security, and so he could understand better the discouragement and despair of many people who came to him with tragic stories.

Care of the soul doesn't mean wallowing in the symptom, but it does mean trying to learn from depression what qualities the soul needs. Even further, it attempts to weave those depressive qualities into the fabric of life so that the aesthetics of Saturn—coldness, isolation, darkness, emptiness—makes a contribution to the texture of everyday life. In learning from depression, a person might dress in Saturn's black to mimic his mood. He might go on a trip alone as a response to a saturnine feeling. He might build a grotto in his yard as a place of saturnine retreat. Or, more internally, he might let his depressive thoughts and feelings just be. All of these actions would be a positive response to a visitation of Saturn's depressive emotion. They would be concrete ways to care for the soul in its darker beauty. In so doing, we might find a way into the mystery of this emptiness of the heart. We might also discover that depression has its own angel, a guiding spirit whose job it is to carry the soul away to its remote places where it finds unique insight and enjoys a special vision.

CHAPTER EIGHT

The Body's Poetics of Illness

THE HUMAN BODY IS AN IMMENSE SOURCE OF IMAGINATION, a field on which imagination plays wantonly. The body is the soul presented in its richest and most expressive form. In the body, we see the soul articulated in gesture, dress, movement, shape, physiognomy, temperature, skin eruptions, tics, diseases . . . in countless expressive forms.

Artists have attempted to convey the expressive powers of the body in many different ways, from odalisques to formal portraits, from Rubens' flesh tones to cubist geometries. Modern medicine, on the other hand, is hell-bent on cure and has no interest in the body's inherent art. It wants to eradicate all anomalies before there is a chance to read them for their meaning. It abstracts the body into chemistries and anatomies so that the expressive body is hidden behind graphs, charts, numbers, and structural diagrams. Imagine a medical approach more in tune with art, one that is interested in the symbolic and poetic suggestiveness of a disease or a malfunctioning organ.

I had a conversation once with a nutritionist about cholesterol that raised some of these issues. Personally, I have felt a strong resistance to making concern about cholesterol the end-all factor in my relationship to my heart and to food. I told her about my misgivings.

"But cholesterol is a major problem," she said. "People who have had heart problems should especially understand the importance of controlling cholesterol in their diets."

Relationship of organs of the body, the humours and the Zodiac,
from Margarita Philosophica, Basel, 1508.

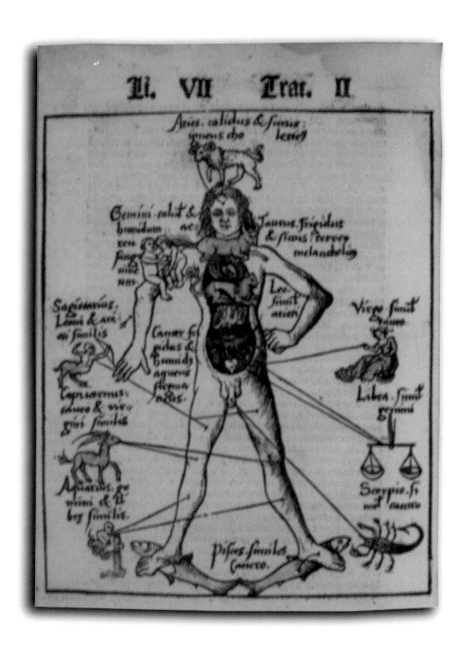

"I don't doubt that cholesterol is a fact," I said, "but I wonder if we take it too factually."

"And the amazing thing is," she went on, "that aspirin can control its bad effects . . . just one every other day."

"Do you recommend that we all take an aspirin regularly for cholesterol?"

"If you have high cholesterol or if you have had heart problems, yes," she said with conviction.

"Why?" I asked.

"So you live longer," she said.

"So, fighting cholesterol is a move against death."

"Yes."

"Is it a denial of death?" I asked more pointedly. "I remember Ivan Illich's statement that he doesn't want to die of some disease. He wants to die of death."

"Maybe it *is* a denial of death."

"Is it possible," I asked, "to appreciate that we have a problem with cholesterol and yet imagine it differently, so that it isn't another way of wrestling with mortality?"

"I have no idea," she said. "There are certain assumptions we make, and we don't question them."

That is the problem with the body. We have certain assumptions we don't reflect on. If we were to reflect, we might imagine cholesterol differently.

The Mask
by Navyo, 1988.

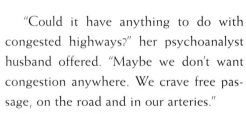

"Could it have anything to do with congested highways?" her psychoanalyst husband offered. "Maybe we don't want congestion anywhere. We crave free passage, on the road and in our arteries."

I appreciated his comment because it took us out of the literal realm of chemistry and treated the symptom as a symbol, a lens through which to see the problem in an altogether different context. This is not to say that congested highways are the *cause* of arterial blockage. Causal thinking usually obstructs imagistic reflection. However, seeing the metaphorical comparison is the beginning of giving the body poetic weight.

Several years ago in Dallas James Hillman gave a lecture on the heart. He was making the point that we are attacking the heart when we treat as a mere physical organ what poetry and song for centuries have treated as the seat of affection. It isn't easy for us, so imbued with modern categories of thought, to remember our own biases in this matter. Of course the heart is a pump. That's a fact. Our problem is that we can't see through the thought structures that give value to fact and at the same time treat poetic reflection as nonessential. In a sense, that point of view is itself a failure of heart. We think with our heads and no longer with our hearts.

Storm in Tropical Forest with Tigers—Surprise! *by Henri Rousseau.*

Hillman's colleague, Robert Sardello, also points out that we give intelligence and power to the brain and then reduce the heart to a muscle. But, he says, the heart has its own intelligence. It knows what to do without orders from the brain. The heart has reasons that may or may not find sympathy from the brain. It has its own style, beating with special force, Sardello notes, in states of passion, as in anger and sex. The brain thinks cool thoughts about cold reality, while the heart thinks in heated rhythms.

Symptoms and Disease

Psychoanalysis has made elaborate attempts to chart connections between psychological experience and physical ailments, but generally both psychology and medicine have been reluctant to read these poetic connections. In the fifteenth century, Marsilio Ficino made the observation that Mars dissolves the intestines. Today, with different language but perhaps with the same insight, we think there is a relationship between repressed anger and colitis. On the whole, however, we have only an unsophisticated understanding of the relationship between a particular physical symptom and the emotions.

Symptom is close to *symbol*. Etymologically a symbol is two things "thrown together," whereas a symptom is things that "fall together," as if by accident. We think that symptoms appear out of nowhere, and we rarely make the move of "throwing together" the two things: illness and image. Science prefers interpretations that are univocal. One reading is all that is desired. Poetry, on the other hand, never wants to stop interpreting. It doesn't seek an end to meaning. A poetic response to disease may seem inadequate in the context of medical science, because science and art differ radically from the point of interpretation. Therefore, a poetic reading of the body as it expresses itself in illness calls for a new appreciation for the laws of imagination, in particular a willingness to let imagination keep moving into ever newer and deeper insights.

Tiger, *from a natural history book, 1801.*

I recently had an experience which in a small way shows the relationship between body and image. I had been feeling a pain in my lower left side. The doctor wasn't sure what it was, but since it didn't worsen over several weeks he suggested watching it closely and not administering any heroic treatments. I agreed completely. Instead, I went to a couple who practice a mild form of massage and who are sensitive to the larger life contexts in which pain presents itself.

It was my first visit, so they asked me some general questions. What do you eat? How is your body doing in general these days? Is there anything going on in your life that you see is related to your pain? If the pain could speak, what might it say?

I appreciated the fact that this session began with a contextualizing of the pain. I found that this simple dialogue had a profound effect on me. It set me in the direction of observing the world surrounding the pain and of listening to its poetics.

Then, as I lay down on the massage table, the two of them, one on each side, began their gentle rubbing. Quickly I fell into deep relaxation. I felt their hands move along my body, slowly and without much pressure. Then I felt fingers on the place of the pain.

Suddenly, several large, brightly colored, imposing tigers leapt out of a cage. They were so close that I couldn't see their entire bodies. Their color was more brilliant than anything that could exist in the natural world. They seemed at once playful and ferocious.

One of the massagers said, "How does it feel when I touch you there?"

I said, "Tigers have arrived."

"Speak to them," she said. "Find out what their message is."

I'd love to have found out, but it was obvious to me these tigers had no interest in speaking English to me. "I don't think they talk," I said.

Even though I was talking to the woman massaging me, the tigers remained playing in the little piece of jungle that had opened up in the dimly lighted room. I didn't make friends with them; they were obviously not about to become pets. But I watched them for quite a while, awed by the strength and brightness of their huge bodies. When the massage was over and the tigers had gone home, I was told that animals frequently make an appearance in that massage room.

I left thinking that I should spend several weeks at least wondering about this visitation. The main things I felt from these tigers were courage, strength, and self-possession, qualities of heart I certainly needed at the time. Not their meaning, but their presence, seemed to give me confidence and strength.

My treatment was less a work to remove pain and more a stimulation of my imagination, so that I could reflect more richly about my body and my life. This is what a symptom is: body and life falling together as if by accident. The response is to contain that coincidence. This could also be a way to read the many androgynous images we find in art and mythology: male and female in one body representing the attempt to contain duality and to live its sometimes grotesque tension. Poetry, whether in literature or in the body, is always demanding that we hold together what seems to belong apart.

A sensitive poetic treatment of images sustains intuition, which is more directly related to emotion and behavioral response than a rational interpretation is. As an added benefit, the images remain intact. My tigers, long after my "treatment," are still a source of wonder and insight for me. Patricia Berry makes an important point about body and images. Images themselves have body, she says, but we, having become so fact-minded, don't appreciate this subtle body of the imagination. We always want to find some corollary in literal life as a way to give an image body . . . a dream must be about what happened during the day. The pain in my side must be from something I ate. It takes a vivid imagination to realize that images have their own bodies. Those tigers were afire with their orange stripes, and their bodies were massive and heavy. As we allow such images their own physical being, we are less inclined to translate them into abstractions.

Bodily Pleasure

If my colon is in pain because of anxiety, then that organ is not just a piece of biologically functioning flesh. It has some link with consciousness and a particular mode of expression. Sandor Ferenczi, Freud's noted Hungarian colleague, described body parts as having their own "organ eroticism." As I understand him, he meant that each organ has its own private life and, you might say, personality that takes pleasure in its activities. My colon was unhappy, and if I could attend to its complaint I might begin to understand what was making it uneasy, or, so to speak, "diseasy." The body's images are like those of a dream. Touch my side and out comes a jungle.

Ferenczi's phrase "organ eroticism" suggests that the body's parts not only function, they also take pleasure in what they do. One asks, not is the organ *working*, but is it enjoying itself. Ferenczi is inviting us to shift the mythic base of our ideas about

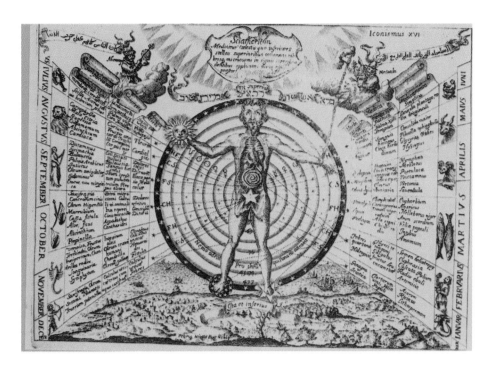

Above: Melothesia, showing Zodiacal signs on the body. *From Ars Magna Lucia et Umbrae Amsterdam 1671. Opposite:* The Four Humours.

body organs from performance to pleasure. I can imagine interviewing my kidneys: Are you relaxed? Are you enjoying your activity today? Or am I doing something that is making you depressed?

A specialist in disease should begin his questions for diagnosis with issues of pleasure. Are you enjoying life? Where is it not pleasurable? Are you fighting pleasure somewhere or in some part of your body that is seeking pleasure?

Whenever pleasure is tied to soul in the writings of philosophers, it is not separated from restraint. Epicurus, as we have seen, lived a simple life and taught a philosophy of pleasure. Ficino, who in his early years espoused the philosophy of Epicurus, explicitly gave a high place to pleasure, yet he was a vegetarian, ate sparsely, traveled none and treasured friends and books over all other possessions. The motto of his Florentine academy was displayed on a banner that read *"pleasure*

Aeschylus and Hygeia, *Roman 5th c. AD.*

in the present." In one of his letters he gave this epicurean advice: "Let your meditation walk no further than pleasure, and even a little behind."

We might imagine much of our current disease as the body asserting itself in a context of cultural numbing. The stomach takes no pleasure in frozen and powdered foods. The back of the neck complains about polyester. The feet die of boredom for lack of walking in interesting places. The brain is depressed to find itself described as a computer and the heart surely doesn't enjoy being treated as a pump. There isn't much opportunity to exercise the spleen these days, and the liver is no longer the seat of passion. All these noble, richly poetic organs, teeming with meaning and power, have been made into functions.

Illness is to a large extent rooted in eternal causes. The Christian doctrine of original sin and the Buddhist Four Noble Truths teach that human life is wounded in its essence, and suffering is in the nature of things. We are wounded simply by participating in human life, by being children of Adam and Eve. To think that the proper or natural state is to be without wounds is an illusion. Any medicine motivated by the fantasy of doing away with woundedness is trying to avoid the human condition.

With this larger dimension in mind, we could examine our lives to see how our actions might be offending the very roots of our existence. We could look for self-contradiction and self-alienation. By discerning the divine principle deep in our activities, we might find the "cure" of our illness. The ancient Greeks taught that the god who heals is the same god who brought the disease in the first place.

Illness's Soul Mate

In his book on Asklepios, the Greek god of medicine, Kerényi reproduces a fascinating ancient sculpture that shows a doctor treating a man's shoulder. In the background, as though in a dream (entirely appropriate to Asklepios, who healed by means of dreams), a snake . . . the god's animal form . . . is touching the man's shoulder with its mouth. This gesture was considered particularly effective for healing. The image suggests that the various treatments physicians employ on the physical plane have counterparts in the soul. In dream, healing is often accomplished by an animal form, not by a rational, technical procedure. As reports of dreams often describe, the snake simply bites the person where it hurts. It vaccinates the patient with its immediate, potentially poisonous contact.

We can learn from this image that all illness is stereophonic. It plays out at the level of actual body tissues and also at the level of dream. All illness is meaningful, although its meaning may never be translatable into entirely rational terms. The following is a dream reported by a sensitive woman trained in the medical professions. She is lying in a bed together with two physicians dressed in white coats. They are talking about a degenerative disease that everyone is going to get. One of the doctors is interested in the fact that in the early stages of the disease, the patient goes deaf. He says that this is an opportunity to experience what it is like to be deaf. Then the scene shifts, and the dreamer walks into the office of another doctor. She sees a porcelain figure of a woman on his desk. She picks it up and holds it to her chest. She notices that the doctor has art objects all around his room. She notices in particular an ivory figurine of a woman with gold-leaf hair and dress. She holds the porcelain figure out and sees that an arm has been broken off at the shoulder, and she feels bad.

Paracelsus.

This dream suggests in several ways the ancient theme of the "wounded healer." The doctors are in bed with the patient. Everyone, including the doctors, will get the disease. One of the doctors even likes the idea of experiencing the symptoms. The patient/dreamer doesn't understand the mysterious truth that illness is unavoidable. How can the problem be treated if everyone is infected? The doctors are not concerned about this issue. They seem to understand and accept the fact that illness is universal.

The dream also shows that whoever cures us has to be "in bed" with our illness. The doctors are not divorcing themselves from the illness, making the patient and her problem something foreign to them. They don't exactly treat it, they become intimate with it, and express the desire to experience it themselves.

Fortunately for the dreamer, the third doctor is like Paracelsus and Ficino. He has art objects in his office. Obviously he knows that medicine is more an art than a science, and that art plays a role in his practice. I am reminded of Freud's office with its celebrated collection of ancient art pieces. As the traditional medicine of many peoples demonstrates, disease can be treated with images. The patient, for her part,

Temple of Music *from Robert Fludd's "Utriusque cosmi Historia," 1617.*

needs to see the images of her healing, just as any of us in distress might look for the stories and images wrapped in our complaints. But she shouldn't bring them too close to her, making them too personal, or they will break apart.

Novalis said, "Every disease is a musical problem. Its cure, a musical solution. The more rapid and complete the solution, the greater the musical talent of the doctor." Many of the ancient physicians I have referred to, such as Robert Fludd and Ficino, were also musicians. They were concerned with the rhythms, tonalities, discords, and concords of the body and the soul. They taught that a doctor, when treating any kind of malady, must know something of the patient's music. What is the tempo of this disease? With what life elements is it in counterpoint? What is the nature of the dissonance that the patient feels as pain and discomfort?

According to Paracelsus, "The disease desires its wife, that is, the medicine. The medicine must be adjusted to the disease, both must be united to form a harmonious whole, just as in the case of man and woman." The dream in which the doctors get into bed with the patient is Paracelsian in tone. The illness is fulfilled and completed by its marriage to treatment. Or, to put it differently, the "wife" . . . the *anima*, image, story or dream . . . of the illness is its medicine.

Above: The Tree *by Odilon Redon.*

Body and Soul

The human body in fifteenth-century Florence was an entirely different body from the one you see in the New York of, say, the 1990s. The modern body is an efficient machine that needs to be kept in shape so that its organs will function smoothly and for as long as possible. If something goes wrong with any part, it can be replaced with a mechanical substitute, because that is the way we picture the body . . . as a machine.

In the Florentine view the human body was a manifestation of the soul. It was possible to entertain a soulless notion of the body, but that was considered an aberration. Such a body was unnaturally split off from soul. We might call it schizoid . . . lifeless, meaningless and without poetics. But an ensouled body takes its life from the world's body, as Ficino said, "The world lives and breathes, and we can draw its spirit into us." What we do to the world's body, we do to our own. We are not masters of this world, we participate in its life.

When we relate to our bodies as having souls, we attend to their beauty, their poetry and their expressiveness. Fortunately, we still have a few institutions that foster an imaginal body. Fashion, for instance, brings a considerable amount of fantasy to the body, although modern dress for men falls quite short in color and variety of styles popular in former times. Cosmetics and perfumery are available to women, and can be an important aspect of cultivating the body's soul.

Exercise could be more soulfully performed by emphasizing fantasy and imagination. Usually we are told how much time to spend at a certain exercise, what heart rate to aim for, and which muscle to focus on for toning. Five hundred years ago Ficino gave somewhat different advice for daily exercise. "You should walk as often as possible among plants that have a wonderful aroma, spending a considerable amount of time every day among such things." His emphasis is on the world and the senses. In a former time, exercise was inseparable from experiencing the world, walking through it, smelling it and feeling it sensually, even as the heart got its massage from the exertion of the walk. Emerson, a great New England walker, wrote in his essay "Nature": "The greatest delight which the fields and woods minister is the suggestion of an occult relation between man and the vegetable. I am not alone and unacknowledged. They nod to me, and I to them." In this Emersonian exercise program, the soul is involved in the perception of an intimacy between human personality and the world's communing body.

We paint the body, photograph it, dance with it, and decorate it with cosmetics, jewelry, clothes, costumes, tattoos, rings, and watches. We know that the body is a world of imagination, and that is the essence of its soul. We might do more for its health by looking seriously at artworks that reveal some of the body's expressiveness than by taking vitamins or doing exercises. An unimagined body is on its way toward disease.

Our hospitals are generally not equipped to deal with the soul in illness. But it wouldn't take much to change them, because the soul doesn't require expensive technology and highly trained experts. Not long ago a hospital administrator asked me for some ideas about improving the hospital's operations. I recommended a few simple things. Their plan was to let patients read their own charts every day and also be given pamphlets describing the chemical and biological aspects of their diseases. I suggested that rather than being given a chart of temperatures and medications, the patients be encouraged to keep track of their impressions and their emotions during their time in the hospital and, most important, to note their dreams every day. I also recommended setting up an art room where patients could paint, sculpt, and maybe dance their fantasies during treatment. I was thinking more of an art studio than of an art therapy room in the usual sense. I also recommended a time and place where patients could tell stories about their illnesses and hospitalization, certainly not with an expert who would reinforce the technical medical format, but maybe with a real storyteller or someone who would know the importance of letting the soul speak and find its images.

Opposite: Ralph Waldo
Emerson, 1803-1882.
Right: Copy of Greek vase
painting, 5th century BCE.

The word *hospital* comes from *hospis,* which means both "stranger" and "host,"
plus *pito,* meaning "lord" or "powerful one." The hospital is a place where the stranger
can find rest, protection, and care. Maybe the disease is the stranger who comes to
the hospital, and maybe the actual hospital is only the concrete form of our own
capacity to host the alien disease. The Latin *hospis* also means "enemy," and I don't
want to lose this shadow element in disease. Illness is an enemy, but we've already
lived out that myth with conviction. Now may be the time to see illness as the
stranger who needs a place in which to stay and be cared for.

The Renaissance therapist Ficino was equipped with a lute on which he could
play his patient's distemper into art. Keats made an easy career move from medicine
to poetry. Emerson explored the mysteries of illness as a philosopher. The tight hold
that the technical fantasy of life has had on modern consciousness appears to be eas-
ing in some quarters. Maybe there is a chance that the body will be freed from its
identification as a *corpus,* a corpse, and once again feel the flush of soul as it becomes
animated by a new appreciation for its own art.

The Economics of Soul: Work, Money, Failure, and Creativity

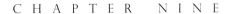

ARE OF THE SOUL REQUIRES ongoing attention to every aspect of life. Essentially it is a cultivation of ordinary things in such a way that soul is nurtured and fostered. Therapy tends to focus on crises or chronic problems. I've never heard anyone come to therapy and say they want to discuss gardening or to examine the soul issues in a house that they're building or to prepare to be a city councilperson. Yet all of these ordinary things have a great deal to do with the condition of the soul. If we do not tend the soul consciously and artfully, then its issues remain largely unconscious, uncultivated, and therefore often problematic.

One of the most unconscious of our daily activities from the perspective of the soul is work and the settings of work—the office, factory, store, studio, or home. I

Night Hawks by Edward Hopper.

have found in my practice over the years that the conditions of work have at least as much to do with disturbances of soul as marriage and family. Yet it is tempting simply to make adjustments in response to problems at work without recognizing the deep issues involved. Certainly we allow the workplace to be dominated by function and efficiency, thereby leaving us open to the complaints of neglected soul. We could benefit psychologically from a heightened consciousness about the poetry of work—its style, tools, timing, and environment.

Several years ago I gave a lecture on the medieval idea that the world is a book to be read. Monks used the phrase *liber mundi*, the "book of the world," to describe a spiritual kind of literacy. Afterward, a woman, a housewife, who had attended telephoned to ask if I would come to her house, to read it in this way. I had never done such a thing, but in therapy I had been reading dreams and paintings for years, so the idea was appealing.

Together we walked through the rooms, observing them closely, and quietly discussed our impressions. This "reading" was not an analysis or an interpretation. It was more "dreaming the house onward," to paraphrase an expression of Jung's—"dreaming the dream onward." My idea was to see the house's poetry and alphabet, to understand the gestures it was making in its architecture, colors, furnishings, decorations, and the condition it was in at that particular time. The woman was truly devoted to her home and wanted to give housework a place of dignity in her life.

Some of the images that came to us were personal. I heard stories of a former marriage, of children, visitors, and her own childhood. Others had to do with the architecture of the building and with American history, and a few touched on philosophical questions about the very nature of dwelling and shelter.

At the end of our tour, we both felt unusually connected to the place and to its things. For my part, I was motivated to reflect on my own home and to think more deeply about the poetics of everyday life.

The home is a place of daily work, whether or not one has an "outside" job. If you were to read your own house, at some point you would find yourself standing before the tools of housework: vacuum cleaner, broom, dustmop, soaps, sponges, dishpan,

Dining Room in the Country *by Pierre Bonnard, 1867–1947.*

hammer, screwdriver. These things are very simple, and yet they are fundamental to the feeling we have of being at home.

I might put it this way: there are gods of the house, and our daily work is a way of acknowledging these home spirits that are so important in sustaining our lives. To them, a scrub brush is a sacramental object, and when we use this implement with care we are giving something to the soul. We can "read" the house of our outside work life in the same way I read that woman's home: examine its environment, look close-

Workers in Amsterdam, *19th c. Right:* Plough *from 19th c. farming catalogue.*

ly at its tools, consider the way time is spent and note the moods and emotions that typically surround the work itself. How you spend your working hours—what you look at, sit on and work with—makes a difference, not only in terms of efficiency but for its effect on your sense of yourself and the direction your imagination takes.

Work as Opus

In many religious traditions, work is not set off from the precincts of the sacred. It is not "pro-fane"—in front of the temple—it is *in* the temple. In Christian and Zen monasteries, for instance, work is as much a part of the monk's carefully designed life as are prayer, meditation, and liturgy. I learned this when I was a novice in a religious order. A novice is a fledgling monk, learning the ins and outs of the spiritual life of prayer, meditation, study, and . . . work. I recall one day in particular, when I was given the job of pruning apple trees. It was a cold day in Wisconsin, and I was out on a limb sawing away at shoots sticking up on limbs all around me like minarets. I took a minute to rest, hoping the limb wouldn't suddenly break, and asked myself, "Why am I doing this? I'm supposed to be learning prayer, meditation, Latin, and Gregorian chant. But here I am, my hands frostbitten, feeling not terribly secure in the top of a tree, my fingers bloody from an erratic sawblade, doing something I know nothing about." The answer, I already knew, was that work is an important component of the spiritual life. In some monasteries monks file off to work in procession, wearing their long hooded robes and maintaining silence. Monastic writers describe work as a path to holiness.

Etymology, the examination of the deep imagery and myth that reside within ordinary language, also offers some insight into work.

Sometimes we refer to work as an "occupation," an interesting word that means "to be taken and seized." In the past this word had strong sexual connotations. We like to think that we have chosen our work, but it could be more accurate to say that our work has found us. Most people can tell fate-filled stories of how they happen to be in their current "occupation." These stories tell how the work came to occupy them, to take residence. Work is a vocation: we are called to it. But we are also loved by our work. It can excite us, comfort us, and make us feel fulfilled, just as a lover can. Soul and the erotic are always together. If our work doesn't have an erotic tone to it, then it probably lacks soul as well.

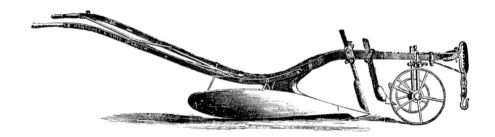

The technical name for the category of rituals that take place in church, such as baptism or the eucharist, is liturgy. It comes from the Greek words *laos* and *ergos*, which together can be translated simply as "ordinary person's work" or "the labor of the laity." The rituals that take place in church are a kind of work, the soul's work: something of the soul is being created in the work of ritual. Still, there is no need to separate that work from the work that goes on "in the world." From a depth point of view, all work is liturgy. We could say, then, that all work is sacred, whether you are building a road, cutting a person's hair, or taking out the garbage.

We can bridge the gap between sacred church and secular world by occasionally ritualizing the everyday things we do. It isn't necessary to place a cloak of religiosity on everyday work in order to make it sacred; formal ritual is only a way of reminding ourselves of the ritual qualities that are in work anyway. Therefore, like a sacristan who reverences everything he tends, we might want to buy tools of satisfying quality—well made, pleasing to look at, and fitted to the hand—and cleansers that respect the environment. A special table cloth might help ritualize a dinner, or an office desk of special design or select woods could transform the workplace into an arena that has imaginal depth. Often work spaces are devoid of imagination, so that the workers are left with a purely secularized feeling that doesn't feed their souls.

Mythology also offers some suggestions for thinking deeply about work. Daedalus, for instance, was known as the ingenious maker of dolls and toys, which came to life when a child played with them. Hephaistos, one of the truly great gods, made furniture and jewelry, among other things, for the other gods. Our own children play with toys as if they were alive, keeping the myth alive. It would make great mythological sense for makers of toys to look deeply into their work and see that Daedalus has a hand in it. If they had a deep sense of the truly magical nature of their product, they could take care of the souls of children with sacred imagination. The same principle holds for all professions and for all forms of labor.

The Lacemaker *by Johannes Vermeer van Delft.*

When we think of work, we only consider function, and so the soul elements are left to chance. Where there is no artfulness about life, there is a weakening of soul. It seems to me that the problem with modern manufacturing is not a lack of efficiency, it is a loss of soul.

Another way to enrich the imagination of work is to follow Jung in his work with alchemy. This process of working the stuff of the soul, objectified in natural materials, the alchemist called the *opus*, that is, "the work." We could imagine our own everyday work alchemically in the same way. The plain concerns of ordinary work are the raw material, the *prima materia*, as the alchemist called it, for working out the soul's matter. We work on the stuff of the soul by means of the things of life. In his book *Psychology and Alchemy*, Jung describes the *opus* as a work of imagination. He is discussing an old alchemical text that tells how to produce the philosophers' stone. The passage says that one should be guided by a true and not a fantastic imagination. Commenting on this idea, Jung says that imagination is "an authentic accomplishment of thought or reflection that does not spin aimless and groundless fantasies into the blue; that is to say, it does not merely play with its object, rather it tries to grasp the inner facts and portray them in images true to their nature. This activity is an *opus*, a work."

Work is an attempt to find an adequate alchemy that both wakens and satisfies the very root of being. Most of us put a great deal of time into work, not only because we have to work so many hours to make a living, but because work is central to the soul's *opus*. We are crafting ourselves—individuating, to use the Jungian term.

To put it more simply, the job and the *opus* are related insofar as work is an extension or reflection of yourself. You conclude a successful business transaction, and you feel good about yourself. You build a cherry dining table or sew a star quilt, then you stand back and contemplate it, feeling a surge of pride. These feelings give a hint that the alchemical *opus* is in play. The trouble is, if what we do or make is not up to our standards and does

The Alchemist, *18th c. colored engraving.*

not reflect attention and care when we stand back to look at it, the soul suffers. The whole society suffers a wound to soul if we allow ourselves to do bad work.

When it is not possible to feel good about our work, then soulful pride, so necessary for creativity, turns into narcissism. Pride and narcissism are not the same thing; in a sense, they are opposites. Like Narcissus, we need to be objectified in an image, something outside ourselves. The products of our work are like the image in

Interior *by Gwen John.*

the pond—a means of loving ourselves. But if those products are not lovable, we are forced into a narcissistic place where we lose sight of the work itself and focus on our own personal needs.

Work becomes narcissistic when we cannot love ourselves through objects in the world. This is one of the deeper implications of the Narcissus myth: the flowering of life depends upon finding a reflection of oneself in the world, and one's work is an important place for that kind of reflection. In the language of Neoplatonism, Narcissus discovers love when he finds that his nature is completed in that part of his soul that is outside himself, in the soul of the world. Read in this way, the story suggests that we will never achieve the flowering of our own natures until we find that piece of ourselves, that lovable twin, which lives in the world and *as* the world. Therefore, finding the right work is like discovering your own soul in the world.

I once counseled a man who worked in an automobile factory. He hated his work. On a team that did spray painting, he was the troubleshooter, clearing up clogged pipes and keeping the chemical mixtures in proper proportion. He was good at what he did, but he experienced his job as an imprisonment. He came to me wondering what had happened in his childhood to make his life so unhappy.

As he talked I noticed that most of his annoyance was focused around his job. So, we discussed his work in detail. Some of his dreams were set on the job site, so we had many occasions to explore the history of his imagination of work, including his childhood fantasies of a life work, his many jobs, his education and training, and his current habits of work. Eventually his reflections on work led him to seek a change. One day he got up enough courage to get a position in sales, which he felt was much better suited to him. Soon many of his "psychological" problems began to disappear. "I love my job," he told me. "I don't mind being criticized for a mistake, and I love to come to work. That other job just wasn't me." The job of troubleshooting spraying operations might have suited another person, but not this man, who had to suffer awhile in his work until he moved into something soulful for him.

In his *Lives of Artists*, Vasari tells a story about the Renaissance sculptor and architect Filippo Brunelleschi. Donatello, Filippo, and other artists were hanging out in

Florence when Donatello mentioned a beautiful marble sarcophagus he had seen in the town of Cortona, a good distance away. "Filippo conceived a tremendous desire to see the work," Vasari writes. "So, without changing his shoes or clothes, immediately he headed off for Cortona, examined the sarcophagus, made a sketch of it, and brought it back to Florence before he was missed." Similar stories are told of Bach walking many miles to hear great music and spending late nights copying the works of composers he admired.

Stories of artists' intensive pursuit of their vision and craft are a kind of mythology revealing the archetypal dimensions of soulful work. In our own lives this archetype may appear in a small way, as in a great feeling of satisfaction after spending the morning at the right task. Or it may appear, as it did for the factory worker, in a satisfying career move. One can imagine a radical restructuring of career counseling toward focusing on the soul. Testing would then assess the nature of the *opus* rather than aptitude, and discussion would touch upon issues much deeper than the surface ego concerns of life.

Money

Money and work are, of course, intimately related. By splitting concern for financial profit from the inherent values of work, money can become the focus of a job's narcissism. In other words, pleasure in money can take the place of pleasure in work. Still, we all require money, and money can be an integral part of work without loss of soul. The crucial point is our attitude. In most work there can be a close relationship between caring for the world in which we live (ecology) and caring for the quality of our way of life (economy).

Ecology and economy, both from the Greek *oikos*, have to do with "house" in the broadest sense. Ecology (*logos*) concerns our understanding of the earth as our home and our search for appropriate ways to dwell on it. Economy (*nomos*) is concerned with the ways in which we get along in this world home and with the family of soci-

The Money Lenders *by Massys.*

ety. Money is simply the coinage of our relationship to the community and environment in which we live. We are paid for our work, and in turn we pay for servic-
es and products. We pay our taxes, and the government provides for the basic needs
of the community. *Nomos* in economics means law, but not natural law. It is the
recognition that community is necessary and that it requires rules of participation.
Money is central in our attempts to live a communal life.

The *experience* of wealth is a subjective thing. For some, to be wealthy is to have credit cards paid off, for others it requires owning a Rolls-Royce or two. Wealth cannot be measured by a bank account because it is primarily what we imagine it to be. Ignorant of the soul and its own brand of wealth, we may become giddy in the pursuit of money because we fear literal poverty around the corner.

In religious orders, monks take a vow of poverty, but if you visit monasteries you might be surprised at how often you find beautifully built and furnished buildings on prime real estate. The monks may live simply but not always austerely, and they never have to worry for food and shelter. Monastic poverty is sometimes defined not as a scarcity of money and property but rather as "common ownership." The purpose of the vow is to promote community by owning all things in common.

What if, as a nation, a city, or a neighborhood, to say nothing of the globe, we all took such a vow of poverty? We would not be romanticizing deprivation, we would be striving toward a deep sense of community by feeling ownership of common property. As it is, we divide property literally into public and private.

The truly wealthy person, however, is the one who "owns" it all—land, air, and sea. At the same time, not splitting wealth and poverty, this wealthy person doesn't own anything. From the perspective of soul, wealth and poverty come together in responsible use and enjoyment of this world, which is only leased to us for the period of our tenure here.

Money is like sex. Some people believe that the more sexual experiences they have, with as many different people as possible, the more fulfilled they will be. But even great quantities of money and sex may not satisfy the craving. The problem lies not in having too much or too little, but in taking money literally, as a fetish rather than as a medium. If wealth is found by rejecting the experience of poverty, then it will never be complete. The soul is nurtured by want as much as by plenty.

Like sex, money is so numinous, so filled with fantasy and emotion and resistant to rational guidance, that although it has much to offer, it can easily swamp the soul and carry consciousness off into compulsion and obsession. We have to distinguish between shadow qualities of money that are part of its soulfulness and symptoms of money gone berserk. We act out the need for wealth of soul through its fetish, gath-

Heavenly Queen in the philosopher's garden
squanderering her endlessly multiplying gold, *Alchemical Treatise, 18th c.*

ering actual sums of money without regard for morality, rather than entering the
communal exchange of money.

It is the nature of money to be exchanged. In fact, we sometimes refer to it as
"change." Robert Sardello, who has studied the role of money in the cultural psyche,
compares economics to bodily processes. Profit and consumption are like breathing
in and out, he says, and money the medium for that vital action in the body of society. When money no longer serves community exchange, it becomes an obstacle to
the communal flow. Scheming and greedy manipulation interfere with the natural
rhythm of exchange. Money is notoriously drenched in shadow, but when any individual or group takes that shadow to themselves, soul is lost.

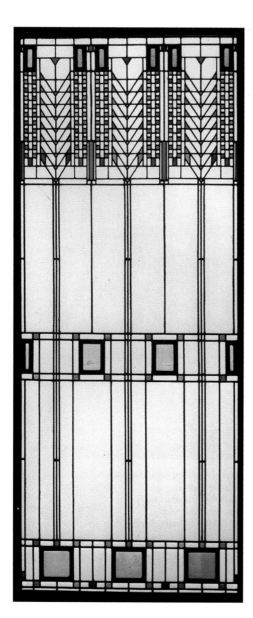

Window *by Frank Lloyd Wright.*

Ideally, money corrupts us all not literally, but in the alchemical sense. It darkens innocence and continually initiates us into the gritty realities of financial exchange. It brings us into hand-to-hand combat in the sacred warfare of life. It takes us out of innocent idealism and brings us into the deeper, more soulful places where power, prestige, and self-worth are hammered out through substantial involvement in the making of culture. Therefore, money can give grounding and grit to a soul that otherwise might fade in the soft pastels of innocence.

Dreams of money often hint at its many levels of meaning. Recently I dreamed I was walking down a dark city street in the early hours of the morning. A man approached me and pressed a knife against my back. "Give me your change," he said. I knew I had two hundred dollars in my right-hand pants pocket and about fifteen in my left. Cleverly I reached into my left pocket and gave him everything that was there. I wondered if he would ask for more, but he took the small sum and ran off. The dark street, a strong image in the dream, was asking me for change. I had noticed in the dream the careful use of that word *change*. Was I being asked to change my ways? To engage in the exchange of the city's darkness? To give something of real value to my own needy shadow side? Do I also hold back my wealth with a false sense of cleverness, with too much thought? In the dream, without hesitating I found a way to outwit the dark street with my duplicity—my *two* pockets.

This dream, I think, gave me needed instruction in the economics of the soul. Money is its coinage and may take the form of passion, energy, talent, or commitment. Like many people, I may hoard my talents, my soul money, for fear of the shadowy streets of embodied life. I may divide my resources, hoarding the greater share while at the same time being prepared to lose small quantities. As is often the case, my dream invited me to consider aspects of my character that I'd prefer to keep hidden and unexamined.

With regard to money's shadow, it's important to be neither moralistic nor literal. For example, the pleasure of hoarding can be seen as an archetypal quality of money itself, which becomes soul-denying only when it is the only way we deal with money, or when we use it for purely personal reasons. One of the things one does with money is to gather it together and hold it: this is the "breathing in" in Sardello's image. If shadow is not acknowledged, however, the hoarding may be carried out with feelings of guilt, a sign that we are trying to do two things at once—enjoy money's hoarding shadow and yet maintain innocence.

Failure in Work

One perhaps surprising source of potential soul in our work is failure. The dark cloud of failure that shadows our earnest efforts is to some extent an antidote for overly high expectations. Our ambition for success and perfection in work drives us on, while worries about failure keep us tied to the soul in the work. When ideas of perfection dive downward into the lower region of the soul, out of that gesture of incarnation comes human achievement. We may feel crushed by failure, but our lofty aims may need some spoiling if they are to play a creative role in human life. Perfection belongs to an imaginary world. According to traditional teaching, it is the life-embedded soul, not soaring spirit, that defines humanity.

According to the alchemists, *mortificatio*, which means "making death," is an important part of the *opus*. Jung explains that mortifications in life are necessary before eternal factors can be manifested. A person is expressing this mystery when he realizes, "It's a good thing after all that I didn't get that job I wanted." For all its simplicity, such a statement penetrates beneath human intention and desire and captures the gist of the mystery of failure. In moments of mortification, you may discover that human intention and ambition are not always the best guides in life and work.

If we do not grasp this alchemy of failure, then we stand a good chance of never succeeding. Comprehending the mystery in failure and acknowledging its necessity—the way it works alchemically on the soul—allows us to see through our inabilities and not overly identify with them. Being literally undone by failure is akin to the "negative narcissism" we examined earlier. It's a negative way of denying the divine or the mysterious a role in human effort. The narcissist says, "I'm a failure. I can't do anything right." But indulgence in failure, wallowing in it rather than letting it affect the heart, is a subtle defense against the corrosive action that is essential to it and that fosters soul. By appreciating failure with imagination, we reconnect it to success.

Creativity with Soul

Creativity, another potential source of soul in our work lives, is much romanticized. Usually we imagine creativity from the *puer* point of view, investing it with idealism and lofty fantasies of exceptional achievement. In this sense, most work is not creative. It is ordinary, repetitious, and democratic.

But if we were to bring our very idea of creativity down to earth, it would not have to be reserved for exceptional individuals or identified with brilliance. In ordinary life creativity means making something for the soul out of every experience. Sometimes we can shape experience into meaningfulness playfully and inventively. At other times, simply holding experience in memory and in reflection allows it to incubate and reveal some of its imagination.

Inside Looking Out *by Ben Shahn.*

Creativity finds its soul when it embraces its shadow. The artist's block, for instance, is a well-known part of the creative process: inspiration stops and the writer is faced with an intractable empty page. Everyone, not only artists, recognizes that evaporation of ideas. A mother may enjoy raising her children for months or years, every day thinking up new ideas for them. Then one day the inspiration leaves and emptiness takes over. If we could see how our blank spots are a part of our creativity, we might not so quickly exclude this aspect of work from our humble lives.

Igor Stravinsky, perhaps the greatest composer of our century, was a hard worker who saw his music less as personal expression and more as an object to be invented and worked. "The workmanship was much better in Bach's time than it is now," he once said in an interview. "One had first to be a craftsman. Now we have only 'talent.' We do not have the absorption in detail, the burying of oneself in craftsmanship to be resurrected a great musician."

Creative work can be exciting, inspiring, and godlike, but it is also quotidian, humdrum, and full of anxieties, frustrations, dead ends, mistakes, and failures. It can be carried on by a person who has none of the soaring Icarus wishes to abandon the dark shadows of the labyrinth in favor of the bright sunshine. It can be free of narcissism and focus on the problems the material world furnishes anyone who wants to make something of it. Creativity is, foremost, being in the world soulfully, for the only thing we truly make, whether in the arts, in culture, or at home, is soul.

As we do our daily work, make our homes and marriages, raise our children, and fabricate a culture, we are all being creative. Entering our fate with generous attentiveness and care, we enjoy a soulful kind of creativity that may or may not have the brilliance of the work of great artists.

The ultimate work, then, is an engagement with soul, responding to the demands of fate and tending the details of life as it presents itself. We may get to a point where our external labors and the *opus* of the soul are one and the same, inseparable. Then the satisfactions of our work will be deep and long lasting, undone neither by failures nor by flashes of success.

III

SPIRITUAL PRACTICE AND PSYCHOLOGICAL DEPTH

Recognize what is before your eyes,
and what is hidden will be revealed to you.

—The Gospel of Thomas ·

CHAPTER TEN

The Need for Myth, Ritual, and a Spiritual Life

I HAVE BEEN EMPHASIZING THE SOUL'S NEED for vernacular life—its relationship to a local place and culture. It has a preference for details and particulars, intimacy and involvement, attachment and rootedness. Like an animal, the soul feeds on whatever life grows in its immediate environment. To the soul, the ordinary is sacred and the everyday is the primary source of religion. But there is another side to this issue. The soul also needs spirituality, and as Ficino advises, a particular kind of spirituality: one that is not at odds with the everyday and the lowly.

In the modern world we tend to separate psychology from religion. We like to think that emotional problems have to do with the family, childhood, and trauma—with personal life but not with spirituality. We don't diagnose an emotional seizure as "loss of religious sensibility" or "lack of spiritual awareness." Yet it is obvious that the soul, seat of the deepest emotions, can benefit greatly from the gifts of a vivid spiritual life and can suffer when it is deprived of them. The soul, for example, needs an articulated worldview, a carefully worked out scheme of values, and a sense of relatedness to the whole. It needs a myth of immortality and an attitude toward death. It also thrives on spirituality that is not so transcendent, such as the spirit of family, arising from traditions and values that have been part of the family for generations.

A client of mine who had trouble with food told me a dream of old women cooking up a hearty outdoor meal. Although this dream was rele-

The River of Life *by William Blake, 1805.*

vant to the young woman's physical problems with food, I thought it also spoke to the hunger in her soul for primordial femininity. By eating the food cooked by the women, she would absorb their spirit; the dream was a female version of the male Last Supper. In another dream related to food, she discovered that her esophagus was made of plastic and wasn't long enough to reach her stomach.

This extraordinary image is a perfect description of one of the main problems of the modern world: our means of connecting to our inner work do not reach deep enough. The esophagus is an excellent image of one of the soul's chief functions: to transfer material of the outside world into the interior. But in this dream it is made of an unnatural substance that stands for the superficiality of our age, plastic. And if this soul function is plastic, then we will not be fed well. We will feel the need of a more genuine means of bringing outer experience deep inside us.

A person starving herself anorectically evokes in her food rituals vestigial forms of religious practice. Her disdain for her body and her asceticism in denying herself food represent pseudoreligion and symptomatic spirituality. A degree of asceticism is a necessary part of spirituality, but a symptomatic, compulsive approach to the ascetic life only shows how far we are from true religious feeling. As society's symptom, anorexia could be trying to teach us that we need a more genuine spiritual life where restraint has a place, but not as neurosis. If our spirituality is like a plastic esophagus, then we are starving ourselves, not fasting in a sacred sense.

In many religions, food is a powerful metaphor. Communion, union with divinity, is accomplished by means of food. Taking food into the body is a ritual way of absorbing the god into oneself. In this context, the woman's dream is especially poignant, since her plastic esophagus interferes with the rite of communion.

All eating is communion, feeding the soul as well as the body. Our cultural habit of eating "fast food" reflects our current belief that all we need to take into ourselves, both literally and figuratively, is plain food, not food of real substance and not the imagination of real dining. Culturally we have a plastic esophagus, suited perhaps to fast food and fast living, but not conducive to soul, which thrives only when life is taken in in a long, slow process of digestion and absorption.

Psychological Modernism

Professional psychology has created a catalogue of disorders, known as the DSM-III, which is used by doctors and insurance companies to help diagnose and standardize problems of emotional life and behavior with precision. For example, there is a category called "adjustment disorders." The problem is that adjusting to life, while perhaps sane to all outward appearances, may sometimes be detrimental to the soul. One day I would like to make up my own DSM-III with a list of "disorders" I have seen in my practice. For example, I would want to include the diagnosis "psychological modernism," an uncritical acceptance of the values of the modern world. It includes blind faith in technology, inordinate attachment to material gadgets and conveniences, uncritical acceptance of the march of scientific progress, devotion to the electronic media, and a life-style dictated by advertising. This orientation toward life also tends toward a mechanistic and rationalistic understanding of matters of the heart.

In this modernist syndrome, technology becomes the root metaphor for dealing with psychological problems. A modern person comes into therapy and says, "Look, I don't want any long-term analysis. If something is broken, let's fix it. Tell me what I have to do, and I'll do it." Such a person is rejecting out of hand the possibility that the source of a problem in a relationship, for example, may be a weak sense of values or failure to come to grips with mortality. There is no model for this kind of thinking in modern life, where almost no time is given to reflection and where the assumption is that the psyche has spare parts, an owner's manual, and well-trained mechanics called therapists. Philosophy lies at the base of every life problem, but it takes soul to reflect on one's own life with genuine philosophical seriousness.

The modernist syndrome also tends to literalize everything it touches. For example, ancient philosophers and theologians taught that the world is a cosmic animal, a unified organism with its own living body and soul. Today we literalize that philosophy in the idea of the global village. The world soul today is created not by a demiurge or semi-divine

Christina's World *by Andrew Wyeth.*

creator as in ancient times, but by fiber optics. In the rural area where I live you can see huge television reception dishes in the backyards of small homes, keeping villagers and country folk tuned into every entertainment and sports event on the earth. We have a spiritual longing for community and relatedness and for a cosmic vision, but we go after them with literal hardware instead of with sensitivity of the heart. We want to know all about peoples from far away places, but we don't want to feel emotionally connected to them.

Retreat from the Modern World

In the past, people concerned with soul often dealt with these problems of the modern world, which to some degree have long been with us, by seeking out a place of retreat. Jung provides a remarkable example of a person attuned to the soul who adjusted his life not to social reality, but to his feelings of longing and restlessness. In his memoirs he tells how he built a stone tower as a dwelling for himself. It began as a primitive structure and over many years grew into something more complicated. He says he didn't have an overall plan in mind from the beginning, but he found out that every four years he added to the building. Significantly, to Jung the number four symbolized wholeness. In the end this tower became a sacred space, a place for his soul work where he could paint on the walls, write his dreams, think his thoughts, enjoy his memories, and record his visions. The title of his memoirs, *Memories, Dreams, Reflections,* reveals the kind of work he accomplished in his tower retreat.

"I have done without electricity," he writes, "and tend the fireplace and stove myself. Evenings, I light the old lamps. There is no running water, and I pump the water from the well. I chop the wood and cook the food. These simple acts make man simple; and how difficult it is to be simple."

Jung's Tower at Kushnacht.

Jung's tower was a personal temple for his spiritual life. Any of us could follow his example and dedicate a room or even a corner of the house for soul work. Jung's tower helped him create a certain kind of space where he could concretely feel his personal lifetime stretched at both ends, reflectively back into the past and prophetically into the future. His tower was a concrete work of imagination that gave him an exit from modern culture. It is one thing to wish for a way beyond the limits of modernism and another to find an effective means of establishing such an awareness; an effective technology of the soul can be crucial.

Jung remarked that in his tower he felt close to his ancestors—another traditional concern of spirituality. "In the winter of 1955-56," he writes, "I chiseled the names of my paternal ancestors on three stone tablets and placed them in the courtyard of the Tower. I painted the ceiling with motifs from my own and my wife's arms. When I was working on the stone tablets, I became aware of the fateful links between me and my ancestors. I feel very strongly that I am under the influence of things or questions

A Hilly Scene *by Samuel Palmer, 1826–1881.*

which were left incomplete and unanswered by my parents and grandparents and more distant ancestors."

This remarkable passage demonstrates how much Jung's inner and outer worlds were in fruitful dialogue with each other. For him, to care for the soul meant building, painting, and carving. His tower stands as the embodiment of his inner urgency for simplicity and eternity.

Getting away from the world has always been part of the spiritual life. Monks secluded themselves in monasteries, ascetics went into the desert, Native American initiates go off on vision quests. Jung's architectural retreat is another version of this archetypal theme—withdrawal from the world. I am not recommending going off to a monastery as a way of dealing with the modernist syndrome that so seriously threatens the life of the soul. Retreat itself can either be soulful or escapist. Some concrete, physical expression of retreat, however, could be the beginning of a spiritual life that would nourish the soul. It could take the modest form of a drawer where dreams and thoughts are kept. It could consist of five minutes in the morning dedicated to writing down the night's dream or to reflect on the day ahead. It might be the decision to take a walk through the woods instead of touring the shopping mall. It might be keeping the television set in a closet, so that watching it becomes a special occasion. It could be the purchase of a piece of sacred art that helps focus attention on spirituality. I know a neighborhood where a man leads a small group doing t'ai chi every morning in a small park.

These are modest forms of retreat that serve the spiritual needs of the soul. Spirituality need not be grandiose in its ceremonials. Indeed, the soul might benefit most when its spiritual life is performed in the context it favors—ordinary daily vernacular life. But spirituality does demand attention, mindfulness, regularity, and devotion. It asks for some small measure of withdrawal from a world set up to ignore soul.

The Rediscovery of Spirituality

Another aspect of modern life is a loss of formal religious practice in many people's lives, which is not only a threat to spirituality as such, but also deprives the soul of valuable symbolic and reflective experience. Care of the soul might include a recovery of formal religion in a way that is both intellectually and emotionally satisfying.

When we look at the history of world religions, in almost every case we see a living tradition. The fundamental insights of every tradition are ever subjected to fresh imagination in a series of "reformations," and what might otherwise be a dead tradition becomes the base of a continually renewing spiritual sensibility.

My own experience bears witness to this pattern of religious reformation. I was brought up in a fervent Irish-Catholic family. I'm sure I was in first grade when the nuns decided I was good material for the priesthood. I did what I was told and got good grades. I became an altar boy, which placed me in close contact with the priests. Often in my grade school years I served as an altar boy at funerals and then ate breakfast with the priest before riding to the cemetery. I was being prepared in subtle ways, and it seemed only natural to leave home at thirteen to enter a prep seminary.

I spent many years then singing Gregorian chant, meditating, and studying theology. I lived the religious life happily, not too worried about celibacy or not having a bank account. Following the will of my superiors was the most difficult thing. But my studies in theology were quite progressive. I was reading Paul Tillich and Teilhard de Chardin more passionately than the typical seminary textbooks. My own theological views were reformed so much, in fact, during my last years of study that shortly before I was to be ordained I decided it was time for a major change. It was the late sixties and revolutionary thought was in the air. I left the seminary with the thought that I would never again regard religion and the priesthood with such devotion.

Not long afterward, I had an odd experience. I had been working in a chemical laboratory for the summer. I wore a white lab coat and mixed concoctions according to coded formulas I was given, but I knew nothing about what I was doing. Around me, however, were true chemists. One evening, at the end of the work day, a brilliant young chemist whom I didn't know well walked with me to the train sta-

The Angelus *by Jean-Francois Millet, 1857.*

tion. We strolled along the tracks and talked about a variety of things. I told him about my seminary training and the new secularism I was enjoying.

He stopped and looked at me closely. "You are always going to do the work of a priest," he said in a strange prophetic tone.

"But I was never actually a priest," I explained.

"No matter," he said. "You will always do the work of a priest."

I didn't know what he was getting at. He was a modern, no-nonsense scientist, yet he was talking like a psychic.

"I don't understand," I said, standing on the tracks. "I've given up on the idea of priesthood. I don't feel any ambivalence. I'm glad to be starting a new life in a new world."

"Don't forget what I'm saying today," he said, and then he changed the subject. I didn't forget.

As the years go by I understand his meaning more and more, although it's still a mystery. After that summer in the lab I went on to study music, but I felt something missing in those old musical scores I had to transcribe by the hour. I wandered for a year or so and then found myself getting a degree in a theology department of a nearby college. One day a professor approached me and suggested that I get a Ph.D. in religion. "But I don't want to study formal religion any longer," I explained patiently.

"I know a place," he said, "Syracuse University, where you can study it the way you want to, with the arts and psychology all woven into it." Three years later I had my degree in religion, and I wondered then if this was what the chemist had in mind. It wasn't the priesthood, but it was close.

Now I find myself a practicing therapist writing about transforming psychotherapy by recovering a religious tradition called care of the soul—which originally was the work of a curate or priest. Even though my current work has nothing explicitly to do with the established church, it is deeply rooted in that tradition. Catholicism is being shaped and lived, for better or worse, in this so-called lapsed—I might say radically reformed—Catholic.

Everyday Sacredness

There are two ways of thinking about church and religion. One is that we go to church in order to be in the presence of the holy, to learn and to have our lives influenced by that presence. The other is that church teaches us directly and symbolically to see the sacred dimension of everyday life. In this latter sense, religion is an "art of memory," a way of sustaining mindfulness about the religion that is inherent in everything we do. For some, religion is a Sunday affair, and they risk dividing life into the holy Sabbath and the secular week. For others, religion is a week-long observance that is inspired and sustained on the Sabbath.

Zen Master Daisetz Suzuki.

I once heard a story about D. T. Suzuki, the early exponent of Zen in the West. He was sitting at a table with a number of distinguished scholars. A man at his side kept asking him questions. Suzuki ate his dinner patiently and said nothing. The man, who obviously had never read a Zen story, then asked: "How would you sum up Zen for a Westerner like me?" With unusual vigor in his voice, Suzuki looked him in the eye and said: "Eat!"

Spirituality is seeded, germinates, sprouts and blossoms in the mundane. It is to be found and nurtured in the smallest of daily activities.

Myth

Amyth is a sacred story set in a time and place outside history, describing in fictional form the fundamental truths of nature and human life. Mythology gives body to the invisible and eternal factors that are always part of life but don't appear in a literal, factual story. Myth reaches beyond the personal to express an imagery reflective of archetypal issues that shape every human life.

In the past few years, a great deal of literature has appeared on the subject of mythology. The strong public response, I believe, has to do with our need for depth and substance in the way we imagine our experience. Mythology from around the world vividly explores the fundamental patterns and themes of human life as you find them anywhere on the globe. The imagery may be specific to the cultures in which the mythology arises, but the issues are universal. This is one of the values of mythology—its way of cutting through personal differences in order to get to the great themes of human experience.

Mythology is not the same as myth. Mythology is a collection of stories that attempt to portray the myths, the deep patterns, that we live in our ordinary lives. Just as stories of our childhood and family evoke the myths that we live as adults, so cultural mythologies evoke mythic patterns that we may trace in modern life.

Mythology teaches us how to imagine more profoundly than sociological or psychological categories allow.

Myth is always a way of imagining; it is not concerned essentially with fact, except that facts can be the starting point for a mythological story. I remember well a guide in Ireland pointing to a rough gap in a mountain ridge and explaining that it was caused by the Devil taking a giant bite out of the land. Mythology often begins with physical evidence, but then uses it as a springboard for fictions, the truth of which concerns human life and values rather than the physical world that spawned the story. We get it backward when we try to trace mythologies back to their physical sources, thinking then that we have explained the myth.

The same principle holds when we try to explain our current feelings and behavior as *caused by* events that happened in the past. Mythological thinking doesn't look for literal causes but rather for more insightful imagining. It considers the past, but the past as myth is different from the past as fact. As myth, the stories we tell about our lives suggest themes and figures that are operative in the present.

The depth of myth is one of its characteristics that make it a useful means for bringing soul into life. As we have seen, soul is at home in a sense of time that reaches beyond the limits of ordinary human life. The soul is interested in eternal issues, even as it is embedded in the particulars of ordinary life. This, the interpenetration of time and eternity, is one of the great mysteries explored by many religions and is itself the subject of many mythologies.

Mythology can also teach us to perceive the myths we are living every day and to observe those that are particularly ours as individuals. Soul work involves an effort toward increasing awareness of these myths that form the foundation of our lives, for if we become familiar with the characters and themes that are central to our myths, we can be free from their compulsions and the blindness that comes upon us when we are caught up in them. Again, we can see the importance of imaginal practices such as journals, dream work, poetry, painting, and therapy aimed at exploring images in dream and life. These methods keep us actively engaged in the mythologies that are the stuff of our own lives.

Ritual

Historically, myth and ritual are in tandem. A people tells its stories of creation and of its deities, and then it worships these deities and celebrates its creation in rites. While mythology is a way of telling stories about felt experience that are not literal, ritual is an action that speaks to the mind and heart but doesn't necessarily make sense in a literal context. In church people do not eat bread in order to feed their bodies but to nourish their souls.

If we could grasp this simple idea, that some actions may not have an effect on actual life but speak instead to the soul, and if we could let go of the dominant role of function in so many things we do, then we might give more to the soul every day. A piece of clothing may be useful, but it may also have special meaning in relation to a theme of the soul. It is worth going to a little trouble to make a dinner a ritual by attending to the symbolic suggestiveness of the food and the way it is presented and eaten. Without this added dimension, which requires some thought, it may seem that life goes on smoothly, but slowly soul is weakened and can make its presence known only in symptoms.

It's worth noting that neurosis, and certainly psychosis, often takes the form of compulsive ritual. People who are severely disturbed chant ritual-sounding words at inappropriate moments or wear exaggerated costumes or wash their hands compulsively. They make gestures with their hands and arms that exaggerate the meanings they want to express. I knew a man who would cross his index fingers whenever he felt the presence of evil, which was several times in an hour, and a woman who would touch her knee at the end of every sentence she spoke.

Could it be that these neurotic rituals appear when imagination has been lost and the soul is no longer cared for? In other words, neurotic rituals could signify a loss of ritual in daily life that, if present, would keep the soul in imagination and away from literalism. Neurosis could be defined as a loss of imagination. We say we "act out," meaning that what should be kept in the realm of image is lived out in life as if it were not poetry. The cure for neurotic ritualism could be the cultivation of a more genuine sense of ritual in our daily life.

Ritual maintains the world's holiness. Knowing that everything we do, no matter how simple, has a halo of imagination around it and can serve the soul enriches life and makes the things around us more precious, more worthy of our protection and care. As in a dream a small object may assume significant meaning, so in a life that is animated with ritual there are no insignificant things. When traditional cultures carve elaborate faces and bodies on their chairs and tools, they are acknowledging the soul in ordinary things, as well as the fact that simple work is also ritual. When we stamp out our mass-made products with functionality blazoned on them but no sign of imagination, we are denying ritual a role in ordinary affairs. We are chasing away the soul that could animate our lives.

I remember the sacred book on the altar when I was a boy, the missal for the Mass. It was bound in red leather, and its pages were marked with colorful, broad, tasseled ribbons. The text was large, and the directions for the liturgy were written in red letters that were a stark contrast to the prayers in black. I can even now take a lesson from these particulars, for instance, to keep in mind the importance of rubrics—the red-lettered instructions that tell precisely how to perform a rite. In my own mind I could give attention every day to rubrics, to the special way things ought to be done.

Naturally, what I am suggesting could be taken in a superficial manner. Sometimes people get caught up in rituals that have no soul. They play with rubrics in too light a manner. I'm talking about a deep sense of how things can be accomplished, with style, to evoke a dimension that truly nourishes the soul. I don't recall much sentimentality in the rituals of the Mass when I was a child. Later, I was taught in theology classes that the rituals are effective *ex opere operato*, "from the thing done," rather than because of the intentions of the one performing the rite. Maybe this is a significant difference between genuine ritual and playing at ritualism—the

Bernard Preaching to Cistercian Monks *from 15th c. painting.*

personal intentions and preferences of the one doing the ritual take second place to the traditions and to the ritual that emerges from the materials themselves.

Rubrics cannot arise out of some superficial place. They may be closely tied to the individual's taste and background, but they must also well up from a solid source deep in the person's psyche. Jung's love for his stone carvings was neither sentimental nor experimental. They had an honesty for him and for us who behold them now much later. But that particular form of ritualizing would not be appropriate for everyone.

How interesting it would be if we could turn to priests, ministers, and rabbis in order to get help in finding our own rubrics and our own ritual materials. These spiritual professionals might be better off becoming deeply schooled in such things rather than trained in sociology, business, and psychology, which seem to be the modern preferences. The soul might be cared for better through our developing a deep life of ritual rather than through many years of counseling for personal behavior and relationships. We might even have a better time of it in such soul matters as love and emotion if we had more ritual in our lives and less psychological adjustment. We confuse purely temporal, personal, and immediate issues with deeper and enduring concerns of the soul.

The soul needs an intense, full-bodied spiritual life as much as and in the same way that the body needs food. That is the teaching and imagery of spiritual masters over centuries. There is no reason to question the wisdom of this idea. But these same masters demonstrate that the spiritual life requires careful attention, because it can be dangerous. The history of our century has shown the proclivity of neurotic spirituality toward psychosis and violence. Spirituality is powerful, and therefore has the potential for evil, as well as for good. The soul needs spirit, but our spirituality also needs soul—deep intelligence, a sensitivity to the symbolic and metaphoric life, genuine community, and attachment to the world.

We have no idea yet of the positive contribution that could be made to us individually and socially by a more soulful religion and theology. Our culture is in need of theological reflection that does not advocate a particular tradition, but tends the soul's need for spiritual direction. In order to accomplish this goal, we must gradually bring soul back to religion, following Jung, who wrote in a letter of 1910 to Freud, "What infinite rapture and wantonness lie dormant in our religion. We must bring to fruition its hymn of love."

Wedding Spirituality and Soul

N O ONE NEEDS TO BE TOLD THAT WE LIVE IN A TIME OF MATERIALISM and consumerism, of lost values and a shift in ethical standards. We find ourselves tempted to call for a return to old values and ways. It seems that in the past we were more religious as a people and that traditional values had more influence throughout the society. But whether or not that is a blurry, nostalgic view of the past, we want to keep in mind Jung's warning about dealing with present difficulties by wishing for a return to former conditions. He calls this maneuver a "regressive restoration of the persona." Societies can fall into this defensive strategy, attempting to restore what is imagined to be a better condition from the past. The trouble is, memory is always part imagination, and tough times of another era are later unconsciously gilded into the "good old days."

If we can resist this temptation to improve the present by restoring the past, we can start to face our current challenges. It appears to me that we are not a society drifting away from spirituality at all; on the contrary, we are in a certain sense more spiritual than we need to be. The key to lost spirituality and numbing materialism is not merely to intensify our quest for spirituality, but to reimagine it.

In the late 1400s, Ficino wrote in his *Book of Life* that spirit and body, religion and world, spirituality and materialism can all be trapped in a polarizing split: the more compulsively materialist we are, the more neurotic our spirituality will be, and vice versa. In other words, perhaps our madly consumerist society is showing signs of runaway spirituality in its tendencies toward an abstract and intellectualized approach to life. Ficino's recommendation for healing such a split is to establish soul in the middle, between spirit and body, as a way to prevent the two from becoming extreme caricatures of themselves. The cure for materialism, then, would be to find

Whirling Dervishes, *from an illuminated Persian manuscript.*

Marsilio Ficino *by Andrea Ferucci, 1521.*

concrete ways of getting soul back into our spiritual practices, our intellectual life, and our emotional and physical engagements with the world.

The pursuit of intellectual and technical knowledge can be undertaken with an excessive fervor or monotheistic single-mindedness sometimes found in the spiritual life. Tracy Kidder's book *The Soul of a New Machine* doesn't really talk about the soul, but it does describe computer inventors and developers as dedicated, self-denying technicians who devote their lives, often to the detriment of their families, to their vision of a technological age. They are "monks of the machine"; caught up in the spirit of their work, like monks of old, they can come to lead an ascetic life in enthusiastic pursuit of a machine that reproduces as much of the natural world as possible in light and electronics. The computer itself, in its refinement of the concrete particulars of life to digital mathematics and light graphics, is, for better or worse, a kind of spiritualization or disembodiment of matter. Medieval monks, too, busied themselves in their own method of sublimating earthly life in intellectual knowledge and reading—copying books and tending to revered libraries.

There are serious drawbacks to the soul in the abstraction of experience. The intellectual attempt to live in a "known" world deprives ordinary life of its unconscious elements, those things we encounter every day but know little about. Jung equates the unconscious with the soul, and so when we try to live fully consciously in an intellectually predictable world, protected from all mysteries and comfortable with conformity, we lose our everyday opportunities for the soulful life. The intellect wants to know; the soul likes to be surprised. Intellect, looking outward, wants enlightenment and the pleasure of a burning enthusiasm. The soul, always drawn inward, seeks contemplation and the more shadowy, mysterious experience of the underworld.

Fundamentalism and Its "Cure"—Polytheism

Often, when spirituality loses its soul, it takes on the shadow-form of fundamentalism. I am not referring to any particular groups or sects, but to a point of view that can seize any of us about anything. One way to describe the nature of fundamentalism is through a musical analogy. If you go to a piano and strike a low C rather hard, you will hear, whether you know it or not, a whole series of tones. You hear the "fundamental" note clearly, but it would sound very strange if it didn't also include its overtones—C's and G's and E's and even B-flat. I would define fundamentalism as a defense against the overtones of life, the richness and polytheism of imagination.

Here we come upon an important rule, applicable to religious spirituality and to stories, dreams, and pictures of all kinds. The intellect wants a summary meaning—all well and good for the purposeful nature of the mind. But the soul craves depth of reflection, many layers of meaning, nuances without end, references and allusions and prefigurations. All these enrich the texture of an image or story and please the soul by giving it much food for rumination.

Ruminating is one of the chief delights of the soul. Early Christian theologians discussed at length how a biblical text could be read at many levels at once. There were literal meanings and allegorical meanings and anagogical (concerned with death and afterlife) meanings. A miracle story may not be a simple proof of Christ's divinity—the soul has little trouble accepting divinity—but may instead express some unfathomable truth about the ways of the soul. Is there a way that the soul can be fed as if with hundreds of loaves and fishes, although in life there is apparently only one of each?

The infinite inner space of a story, whether from religion or from daily life, is its soul. If we deprive sacred stories of their mystery, we are left with the brittle shell of fact, the literalism of a single meaning. But when we allow a story its soul, we can

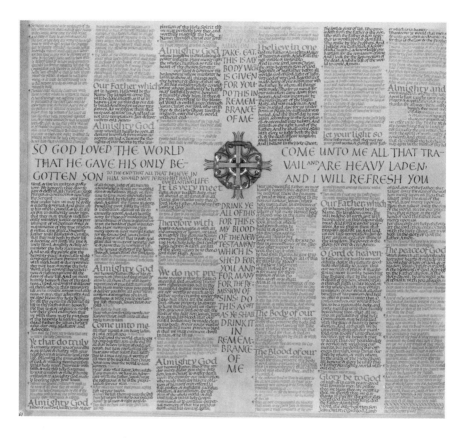

The Communion Service *by Peter Halliday, 1976.*

discover our own depths through it. Fundamentalism tends to idealize and romanti-
cize a story, winnowing out the darker elements of doubt, hopelessness, and emptiness. It protects us from the hard work of finding our own participation in meaning
and developing our own subtle moral values.

I have said that the soul is more interested in particulars than in generalities. That
is true of personal identity as well. Identifying with a group or a syndrome or a diagnosis is giving in to an abstraction. Soul provides a strong sense of individuality—
personal destiny, special influences and background, and unique stories. In the face

of overwhelming need for both emergency and chronic care, the mental health system labels people schizophrenics, alcoholics, and survivors so that it can bring some order to the chaos of life at home and on the street, but each person has a special story to tell, no matter how many common themes it contains.

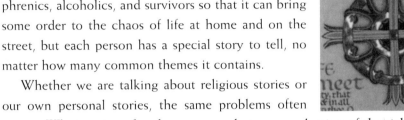

Whether we are talking about religious stories or our own personal stories, the same problems often appear. What we too often hear are conclusions, a reduction of the rich details of a story to some overarching meaning or moral. In Jungian language, we could say we need to find the *anima* in these stories—their living, breathing soul. Bringing soul to a story entails de-moralizing our images, letting them speak for themselves rather than for an ideology that restricts and slants them from the beginning.

The soul's complex means of self-expression is an aspect of its depth and subtlety. When we feel something soulfully, it is sometimes difficult to express that feeling clearly. At a loss for words, we turn to stories and images. Nicholas of Cusa concluded that we often have no alternative but to live with "enigmatic images." Since soul is more concerned with relatedness than intellectual understanding, the knowledge that comes from soul's intimacy with experience is more difficult to articulate than the kind of analysis that can be done at a distance. Soul is also always in process, having, as Heraclitus says, it own principle of movement; so it is difficult to pin down with definition or a fixed meaning. When spirituality loses contact with soul and these values, it can become rigid, simplistic, moralistic, and authoritarian—qualities that betray a loss of soul.

Ingmar Bergman's masterly film *Fanny and Alexander* shows this difference graphically. It contrasts the vitality of family life—colorful relatives, abundant food, festive celebration, mysteries, and shadow—with life under a rigid, authoritarian bishop. The film's mood shifts from fun, intimacy, bawdiness, music, character, belonging, and a warm sense of home to a gray, depressive emphasis on rules, solitude, punishment, fear, emotional distance, violence, and the hope for escape. Obviously, it is not spirituality as such that is presented in the figure of the bishop, but rather a fun-

Thomas More *by Hans Holbein.*

damentalist religious spirit cut off from soul. For even the highest and strictest forms of spirituality can coexist with soulfulness. Thomas Merton, who lived in a hermitage, was known for his humor and laughter. St. Thomas More wore a hairshirt as part of his spiritual practice, yet he was a man of wit, strong family feelings, deep involvement in law and politics, and warm friendship. The problem is never in spirituality in itself, which is absolutely necessary for human life, but the narrow fundamentalism that arises when spirituality and soul are split apart.

There are many different kinds of spirituality. The kind with which we are most familiar is the spirituality of transcendence, the lofty quest for the highest vision, universal moral principles, and liberation from many limitations of human life. Play the child's game of making a church with your fingers. "Here's the church and here's the steeple." There you have a simple image of transcendent spirituality. But "open the door and here are all the people," and you see the inner multiplicity of the soul. This is like the statue Plato describes that on the outside is the face of a man, but once opened up contains all the gods.

Polytheistic religions, which see gods and goddesses everywhere, offer useful guidance toward finding spiritual values in the world. You don't have to be a polytheist in order to expand your spirituality in this way. In Renaissance Italy, leading thinkers who were pious and monotheistic in their Christian devotion still turned to Greek polytheism for a wider range of spirituality.

If we can get past various fundamentalist attitudes about the spiritual life, such as attachment to a too simple code of morality, fixed interpretations of stories, and a community in which individual thinking is not prized, then many different ways of

Triptich in the form of a Madonna and Child, *Germany, 15th c.*

being spiritual come into view. We may discover that there are ways to be spiritual that do not counter the soul's needs for body, individuality, imagination, and exploration. Eventually we might find that all emotions, all human activities, and all spheres of life have deep roots in the mysteries of the soul, and therefore are holy.

The Soul of Formal Religion

Still another way to be spiritual and soulful at the same time is to "hear" the words of formal religion as speaking to and about the soul. Again, Jung gives us an example in his own life. He was fascinated by the dogma of the Assumption of the Virgin Mary, which was proclaimed by the Catholic Church in 1950. No matter that Jung wasn't Catholic. For him this was an important day for the soul, in his words "the most important religious event since the Reformation." It brought woman into the sphere of divinity and signaled a further incarnation of the divine within human life, he thought.

Baptism of Christ *by Pierro della Francesca.*

Formal teachings, rites, and stories of religions provide an inexhaustible source for reflection on the mysteries of the soul. For example, consider the story of Jesus standing in the Jordan River to be baptized as he is about to begin his life work. This scene is a portrait of a significant moment in any life: one finds oneself standing in the powerful, streaming currents of time and fate. Catholic teaching says that the water of baptism has to flow: among other things, it represents the stream of events and persons in which the individual finds his place. Heraclitus used the river as an image of life's currents when he said laconically, "Everything flows."

We read the story of Jesus in the river, whether we are Christian or not, and are inspired to make our own baptism. The Jordan is the archetype of our willingness to live fully, to have our own work and mission, and therefore to be blessed, as the Gospel story tells, by a higher father and a protecting spirit. The Renaissance artist Piero della Francesca painted this scene at the Jordan, showing Jesus standing straight in his full dignity, while in the background another man about to be baptized—any of us taking our turn—has his garment almost off, lifted over his head in a posture of exquisite ordinariness. It's an inspiring image of the willingness to step courageously into the river of existence, instead of finding ways to remain safe, dry, and unaffected.

Religious iconography and architecture also show us how spirituality and soul come together. The great cathedrals of Europe portray spirituality in their soaring steeples and tall pointed windows. The steeples vanish in air, like rockets leaving earth for the cosmos. But these cathedrals are also filled with an abundance of color and carvings, sculptures, tombs, crypts, alcoves, chapels, shrines, images, and sanctuaries—all haunts of soul, places of interiority, reflection, imagination, story, and fantasy. The cathedral could be seen as a union of soul and spirit in which both have equal importance and are inherently related to each other.

Ideas with Soul

In the first graduate course in psychology that I taught the students were disturbed to find original writings of Freud and Jung on the reading list. They came to me and complained that the reading was too difficult. These were mature students, already working in the field, and they were intimidated by the original works of major writers. They had been educated for years with textbooks that systematized and summarized the theories of the founding psychologists. But a textbook is a reduction of subtle thought into a simple outline. In the process of streamlining complicated thought, soul is lost. The beauty of the writings of Freud, Jung, Erickson, Klein, and others lies in their complexity, in the inner contradictions that appear from work to work, and in the personal quirks and biases that are everywhere in the original writings and nowhere in the textbooks. You couldn't find quirkier writers than Freud and Jung, and in their personal styles lies the soul of their work.

Once I was asked to sit in on the oral defense of a master's thesis in psychology. I read the quantitative research paper and found one paragraph, on page ninety-five, devoted to "discussion." During the questioning I asked the student why the discussion of her study was so brief. The rest of the committee looked at me with alarm, and later I was told that the discussion was supposed to be at least that short since "speculation" wasn't to be encouraged. The word *speculation* rang out like an obscenity. Whatever was not firmly grounded in quantitative research was considered speculation and had little value in comparison. To me, though, speculation was a good word, a soul word, coming from *speculum*, mirror, an image of reflection and contemplation. This student had fulfilled the spirit, so to speak, of her topic by doing a careful quantitative study, but she had done little for its soul. She could recite the hard details of her research design, but she couldn't reflect on the deeper issues involved in her study, even though she had spent hundreds of hours gathering data

Remaining in the Middle *by Sat Navyo, 1986.*

Icarus and Daedalus
from Villa Albani,
Rome.

and working up her research. She was rewarded for this, while I was considered out of touch with modern methodology. She passed, but I failed.

The intellect often demands proof that it is on solid ground. The thought of the soul finds its grounding in a different way. It likes persuasion, subtle analysis, an inner logic, and elegance. It enjoys the kind of discussion that is never complete, that ends with a desire for further talk or reading. It is content with uncertainty and wonder. Especially in ethical matters, it probes and questions and continues to reflect even after decisions have been made.

We are not going to have a soulful spirituality until we begin to think in the ways of soul. If we bring only the intellect's modes of thought to our search for a path or to spiritual practices, then from the very beginning we will be without soul. The bias toward spirit is so strong in modern culture that it will take a profound revolution in the very way we think to give our spiritual lives the depth and subtlety that are the gifts of soul. Therefore, a soul-oriented spirituality begins in a reevaluation of the qualities of soul: subtlety, complexity, ripening, worldliness, incompleteness, ambiguity, wonder. In therapy I sometimes hear people say they are overwhelmed by feelings and events too complicated to handle. I think to myself, if only this person could think through his values and arrive at some theories about life in general and his own life in particular, that sense of being overwhelmed might be tempered.

Should I be a vegetarian? Is there ever a just war? Will I ever be free of racial prejudice? How far should I go toward responsibility for the environment? How politically active should I be? Moral reflections like these give rise to a philosophy of life that may never have absolute clarity or simplicity. But these soul thoughts can generate a deep-rooted moral sensitivity, different from a straightforward adherence to an established set of principles, but solid and demanding nonetheless.

Deepening *Puer* Spirituality

In our reflections on narcissism we had the opportunity to look at the attitude and point of view that Jungian and archetypal psychology call *puer*. *Puer* is the face of the soul that is boyish, spirited in a way that is perfectly depicted in the image of a male child or young man.

Because the *puer* attitude is so unattached to things worldly, it isn't surprising to find it prevalent in religion and in the spiritual life. For example, there is the story of Icarus. Icarus was the young man who, escaping the labyrinth, put on waxen wings made by his father Daedalus, then flew (despite his father's warnings) too close to the sun and fell tragically to earth.

One way to understand this story is to see it as the *puer* putting on the wings of spirit and becoming birdlike as a way of getting out of labyrinthine life. His escape is excessive, exceeding the range of the human realm, and so the sun sends him plummeting to his death. The story is an image of spirituality carried out in the *puer* mode. Anyone can turn to religion or spiritual practice as a way out of the twists and turns of ordinary living. We feel the confinement, the humdrum of the everyday, and we hope for a way to transcend it all.

I know, from having lived the monastic life myself, how exhilarating that sense of rising above ordinary life can be, with its feelings of purity and unfetteredness; there are moments when I still long for it.

The vertical movement of the spiritual life is not only freeing, it's also inspiring and, of course, inflating. The feeling of superiority it gives seems worth most of the worldly deprivations required. But the *puer* spirit, so charged with the desire to flee the complexity of the labyrinth, can melt in the heat of its own transcendence. What can only be called a "spiritual neurosis" may develop. I have seen dedicated young men carry self-deprivation too far, suffering the Icarian crash in depressions and obsessions clearly tied to their spiritual aspirations. Some spiritual people effectively leave worldliness behind them, but for others there are dangers in those rarefied airs of spirit. It isn't easy for the high-flying *puer* to remain tethered to soul.

Bellerophon is another boy of myth. He rides the winged horse Pegasus in order to eavesdrop on the conversations of the gods and goddesses, but he falls, too. Here is another *puer* aspect of religion—the desire to know what it is not given to humans to know. Phaethon tries to drive the chariot of the sun across the sky but falls in a fiery crash upon the earth. Acteon, the hunter, wandering into the

The Fall of Icarus *by Pieter Breughel the Elder.*

Acteon torn by his own dogs, 5th c. BCE.

woods, intrudes on Artemis at her bath and is transformed into a deer. He is then hunted down and killed.

I want to avoid any hint of a moralistic tone in presenting the stories of these mythic young men. Punishment in myth need not be read literally. Rather, the idea is that certain actions elicit specific outcomes. There is karma in *puer* spirituality. The suffering peculiar to each *puer* figure is simply the underside of the pattern. If you let your attention wander, as Acteon did, then you might glimpse wondrous sights hidden to ordinary vision, but you also are going to be changed by your good fortune. The punishments in these stories tell that the soul is *affected* by *puer* movements toward divinity. There is no point in avoiding being affected, but perhaps one should know in advance that spiritual vision comes with a price. Jesus has many qualities of the *puer*.

"My kingdom is not of this world," he says again and again. He is an idealist, preaching a doctrine of brotherly love. He also talks about doing his father's work, sustaining the image of himself as a son. He has a vulnerable childhood, and, much in the manner of another young religious idealist, Gautama Buddha, he is tempted by the devil's invitations to power and wealth, but easily brushes aside these claims of the world. He performs miracles that defy natural law—the longing of every *puer*. And, like the *puer* Hamlet, he carries the burden of his father's spiritual charge. He has a melancholy side, epitomized in his agony in the garden. Finally, of course, Jesus is raised vertically, like the *puer* figures of myth, upon the cross where he is shown to have been beaten and to have bled, a typical suffering endured by the *puer*.

The *puer* spirit provides us with fresh vision and necessary idealism. Without it, we would be left with the heavy load of social structures and thinking that isn't adequate for a quickly developing world. At the same time, the *puer* spirit can wound the soul. For example, being so high above ordinary life, whether on wings or horses or chariots, it considers itself invincible. It can be insensitive to the failures and weakness of ordinary mortal life.

There can also be cruelty in the soaring itself. A man once told me a dream in which he was flying a biplane over the farm where he grew up. He could see his family down on the ground in front of the house. They were signaling to him to land and be with them, but he kept flying in circles around them. The *puer* spirit often maintains its distance from the labyrinth of the family. From the soul's point of view, this dream shows a defense against that labyrinth and a choice of pure spirit—air—over descent into the family soul. The family is unhappy and feels the rejection. This theme has its echo in families that try to kidnap and deprogram their children who have joined cults. At issue may be the archetypal struggle of Icarus and Minotaur— the devouring beast at the heart of labyrinthine life that threatens the *puer*. It was said to feed on young men and women.

Once when I was giving a talk on dreams at a spiritualist church, a middle-aged woman in the group told a dream in which she and her family were climbing a mountain. The way was difficult and they had to maneuver over sharp, pointed rocks. At the top, the dreamer found herself hanging onto a thick rope at the end of which dangled her son-in-law, flying high in the air. Even his clothes were puffed up with air. He was "inflated," she said, although she didn't seem to grasp the psychological nuance in the word. She said she was afraid that if she let go of the rope he might fly away and disappear. He himself assured her that he was fine and was having a great time.

At this time in her life she was making an arduous ascent to the spirit, while at the same time she was a mother fully connected to the world through her family. At the end of her struggle she was identified with the mother who fears for the safety of the son-in-law of her own soul. She was afraid to let that spirit go lest it vanish into the air. This woman believed in earth; she could handle *its* requirements. But she was afraid of the heights to which her spirit might soar.

Here we have a twist on our theme: one feels a threat to the soul in a runaway spirit, but real harm can be done by a fearful hanging on to a soaring spirit and weighing it down too much with a heavy sense of earthly responsibility. In the dream, the rope was slack: the young man was enjoying a certain level of flight. He wasn't straining to soar higher. The dreamer misread the situation and found herself as a result in unnecessary anguish. The dream supports my impression that we are a people afraid of the heights to which the spirit might take us and so we turn to forms of religion that temper and contain the spirit that potentially could transform our lives. We go to church as much to subdue that spirit as to acknowledge it. Part of preparing spirit for marriage with soul is to let spirit fly and find its airborne pleasures.

The dreamer couldn't let go of the angel disguised as her son-in-law. She had made her way to the top of the mountain. She had obviously made some real achievements in her spirituality. But at that point she couldn't fathom the mystery of spiritual poverty—letting go of fear, desire, and effort. The man's pants are filled with spirit. They keep him afloat, in a modest ballooning, of human dimensions. He's not in a rocket; he's like a young clown, a spiritual daredevil of an angel.

Faith

Faith is a gift of spirit that allows the soul to remain attached to its own unfolding. When faith is soulful, it is always planted in the soil of wonder and ques-

Pegasus by Alfred Pinkham Ryder.

tioning. It isn't a defensive and anxious holding on to certain objects of belief, because doubt, as its shadow, can be brought into a faith that is fully mature.

Imagine a trust in yourself, or another person, or in life itself, that doesn't need to be proved and demonstrated, that is able to contain uncertainty. People sometimes put their trust in a spiritual leader and are terribly betrayed if that person then fails to live up to ideals. But a real trust of faith would be to decide whether to trust someone, knowing that betrayal is inevitable because life and personality are never without

Cretan wall-painting, 1500 BCE.

shadow. The vulnerability that faith demands could then be matched by an equal trust in oneself, the feeling that one can survive the pain of betrayal.

I've worked with several people who are very devoted to religion and pride themselves on their faith. But they have no trust in themselves, and they don't entrust themselves to life. In fact, they use their belief system to keep life at a distance. Belief can be fixed and unchanging, but faith is almost always a response to the presence of the angel, like the one who stirs the waters.

A cousin of mine who was a nun once confided in me her story of an immense struggle of faith. An early bloomer in spirituality, she had entered the convent young and then spent years living that life enthusiastically. She spent many summers getting degrees in science and then taught science courses in various high schools run by her order. But she also studied Zen Buddhism and Eastern meditation practices in a day when ecumenism was frowned upon. Whatever she was doing or talking about, you could feel in her an extraordinary purity of intention and unlimited commitment.

One day she discovered that she had a rare, painful, and fatal disease. Characteristically, she arranged her life the best way she could. She studied her illness and developed her own regimens of self-care.

Then, in the midst of her illness, the pain and disruption in her life took their full toll. She lost her faith. Everything she had believed in collapsed into a deep, dark hole, and she felt that all her previous efforts to live an honest, principled life had been in vain. She called for a priest, but, rather astonishingly, when she told him about her loss of faith, he dashed out of her room. She said she long remembered the image of his back as he hurriedly pushed open the door to get away from her doubt and depression.

She had no choice then but to sink into her black emotion. She had never thought, in all her studies and training in spirituality, that she could have such a crisis of faith. She had no guides, no hints at where to go next. She had no life in front of her and no one to talk to. She had read about the Eastern concept of emptiness, but she didn't know it could feel so barren.

But, she told me, eventually she discovered a new kind of faith that rose directly out of her depressive thoughts and emotions. She was shocked to feel it stir in that deep, empty pit. She didn't know what to think of it because it was so different from the kind of faith she had been learning about and nurturing all her life. It was inseparable from her illness and her incapacity. Within this new brand of spirituality, however, she uncovered a profound peace. She no longer craved comfort from the hospital chaplain or anyone else. She said she found it difficult to describe this new trust she felt, because it was so deep and different from the faith she had been cultivating in her previous spiritual practices. There was more individuality in this faith; it was tied closer than could be imagined to her own identity and to her illness. She had found what she needed the only way she could—alone. Not long after she told me this story of her loss and recovery of faith, she died peacefully.

There is an economics of the soul by which entry into new areas of thought, emotion, and relationship demands a steep price. Dreams teach this lesson in the imagery of money. The dreamer is told to reach into his pockets and pay the railway conductor or the thief or the shopkeeper. In mythology, the one who journeys to the gate of the underworld is advised to bring some change in order to pay the price of passage. My relative had to pay a high price to the ferryman when she approached his river of forgetfulness. She had to give up her long-held certainties and the joy of her spiritual life. Her former faith had to be emptied before it could be renewed and completed.

The nun's attention had long been focused on her spiritual practice, but then she was forced to look at her own heart without any spiritual props or lenses. She learned, I think, the lesson taught by many mystics: that this necessary dimension of faith is spawned by unknowing. Nicholas of Cusa said we have to be educated into our ignorance or else the full presence of the divine will be kept at bay. We have to arrive at that difficult point where we don't know what is going on or what we can do. That precise point is an opening to true faith.

The Divine Union

In the midst of everyday struggle we hope for enlightenment and some kind of release. In our prayer and meditation, we hope for a fulfilling ordinary life. Jung always taught that these two, *anima* and *animus*, are capable of a mystical wedding, the *hieros gamos*, a divine union. But it is not an easy marriage to effect. Spirit tends to shoot off on its own in ambition, fanaticism, fundamentalism, and perfectionism. Soul gets stuck in its soupy moods, impossible relationships, and obsessive preoccupations. For the marriage to take place, each has to learn to appreciate the other and to be affected by the other—spirit's lofty aims tempered by the soul's lowly limitations, soul's unconsciousness stirred by ideas and imagination.

In spiritual literature the path to God or to perfection is often depicted as an ascent. It may be done in stages, but the goal is apparent, the direction fixed, and the way direct. Images of the soul's path, as we have seen, are quite different. Odysseus is called *"polytropos,"* a man of many turns—a good word for the path of soul. Demeter must seek her daughter everywhere and finally descend to the underworld before earth can come back to life. There is also the odd path of Tristan, who travels on the sea without oar or rudder, making his way by playing his harp.

As the soul makes its unsteady way, delayed by obstacles and distracted by all kinds of charms, aimlessness is not overcome. The wish for progress may have to be set aside. In his poem *"Endymion"* Keats describes this soul path exactly:

> But this is human life: the war, the deeds,
> The disappointment, the anxiety,
> Imagination's struggles, far and nigh,
> All human; bearing in themselves this good,
> That they are still the air, the subtle food,
> To make us feel existence.

This is the "goal" of the soul path—to *feel existence;* not to overcome life's struggles and anxieties, but to know life firsthand, to exist fully in context. On the soul's odyssey, or in its labyrinth, the feeling is that no one has ever gone this way before.

The Fool *from the Marseille Tarot pack*.

People in therapy often ask, "Do you know anyone else who's had this experience?" It would be a relief to know that the blind alleys of this soul path are familiar to others. "Do you think I'm on the right track?" someone else will ask.

But the only thing to do is to be where you are at this moment, sometimes looking about in the full light of consciousness, other times standing comfortably in the deep shadows of mystery and the unknown.

The path of soul is also the path of the fool, the one without pretense of self-knowledge or individuation or certainly perfection. If on this path we have achieved anything, it is the absolute unknowing Cusanus and other mystics write about, or it is the "negative capability" of John Keats—"being in uncertainties, mysteries, doubts, without any irritable reaching after fact and reason."

As we become transparent, revealed for exactly who we are and not who we wish to be, then the mystery of human life as a whole glistens momentarily in a flash of incarnation. Spirituality emanates from the ordinariness of this human life made transparent by lifelong tending to its nature and fate.

Toward the end of *Memories, Dreams, Reflections,* Jung writes, "The whole man is challenged and enters the fray with his total reality. Only then can he become whole and only then can God be born."

Spiritual life does not truly advance by being separated either from the soul or from its intimacy with life. God, as well as man, is fulfilled when God humbles himself to take on human flesh. The theological doctrine of incarnation suggests that God validates human imperfection as having mysterious validity and value. Our depressions, jealousies, narcissism, and failures are not at odds with the spiritual life. Indeed, they are essential to it. When tended, they prevent the spirit from zooming off into the ozone of perfectionism and spiritual pride. More important, they provide their own seeds of spiritual sensibility, which complement those that fall from the stars. The ultimate marriage of spirit and soul, *animus* and *anima,* is the wedding of heaven and earth, our highest ideals and ambitions united with our lowliest symptoms and complaints.

IV

CARE OF THE WORLD'S SOUL

Humility in the artist is his frank acceptance of all experiences,
just as Love in the artist is simply that sense of Beauty that reveals
to the world its body and its soul.

—Oscar Wilde

Beauty and the Reanimation of Things

Wisconsin Farmscene *by Paul A. Seifert, 1880.*

T HE RENAISSANCE MAGUS UNDERSTOOD THAT OUR SOUL, the mystery we glimpse when we look deeply into ourselves, is part of a larger soul, the soul of the world, *anima mundi*. This world soul affects each individual thing, whether natural or human-made. You have a soul, the tree in front of your house has a soul, but so too does the car parked under that tree.

To the modern person who may think of the psyche as a chemical apparatus, the body as a machine, and the manufactured world as a marvel of human brainpower and technology, the idea of *anima mundi* might seem strange indeed. The best some forms of psychology can do with our occasional intuitive sensation that all things are alive is to explain the phenomenon as projection, the unconscious endowment of human fantasy onto an "inanimate" object. *Inanimate* means "without *anima* "—no *anima mundi*.

The trouble with the modern explanation that we *project* life and personality onto things is that it lands us deeply in ego: "All life and character comes from me, from how I understand and imagine experience." It is quite a different approach to allow things themselves to have vitality and personality.

In this sense, care of the soul is a step outside the paradigm of modernism, into something entirely different. My own position changes when I grant the world its soul. Then, as the things of the world present themselves vividly, I watch and listen. I respect them because I am not their creator and controller. They have as much personality and independence as I do.

Everyone knows that we can be deeply affected by the things of nature. A certain hill or mountain can offer a deep emotional focus to a person's life or to a family or community. When my great-grandparents settled in upstate New York after emigrating from Ireland, they created a thriving small farm in the countryside. They raised many kinds of animals, sowed fields with a variety of crops, and planted and tended an orchard with great care. The house that they built was graceful to look at from the outside, and inside it was filled with old paintings and photographs. In front of the house were two grand chestnut trees that offered shade and beauty for the family and the many people who visited the farm for over fifty years.

Not long ago I joined up with some cousins and paid a visit to the old homestead, which had been sold to a man who wanted the land only for hunting. We found that the barn had fallen to the ground and was now completely hidden by brush; even the house was no longer visible among the tall grasses that had grown up around its foundation. But a piece of the orchard was still visible, and the chestnut trees had not lost their nobility and kindliness. My cousins and I talked about those trees and some of the people who had sat under them on hot summer days telling tall tales and innumerable stories about the past.

If someone thinking of widening the road or building a new house should ever come to cut down those chestnut trees, it would be a painful loss for me and many members of my family, not just because the trees are symbols of time past, but because they are living beings filled with beauty and surrounded by a huge aura of memory. In a real sense they are part of the family, bound to us as individuals of another species but not another community.

Made things also have soul. We can become attached to them and find meaningfulness in them, along with deeply felt values and warm memories. A neighbor told me he wanted to move to a different town, but his children loved their house so much they wouldn't let him make the move. We know these feelings of attachment to things, but we tend not to take them seriously and allow them to be part of our worldview. What if we took more seriously this capacity of things to be close to us, to reveal their beauty and expressive subjectivity? The result would be a soul-ecology, a responsibility to the things of the world based on appreciation and relatedness rather than on abstract principle. Our felt relationship to things wouldn't allow us to pollute or to perpetuate ugliness. We couldn't let a beautiful ocean bay become a sewer system for shipping and manufacturing because our hearts would protest this violation of soul. We can only treat badly those things whose souls we disregard.

Let's return to the word *ecology*. As we have already seen, *oikos* means "home." Speaking from the point of view of soul, ecology is not earth science, it is *home* science; it has to do with cultivating a sense of home wherever we are, in whatever context. The things of the world are part of our home environment, and so a soulful ecology is rooted in the feeling that this world is our home and that our responsibility to it comes not from obligation or logic but from true affection.

Without a felt connection to things we become numb to the world and lose that important home and family. The homelessness we see on our city streets is a reflection of a deeper homelessness we feel in our hearts. Homeless people embody a deprivation of soul which we all experience to the extent that we live in an inanimate world without the sense of a world soul to connect us to things. We assume that our loneliness has to do with other people, but it also comes from our estrangement from a world that we have depersonalized by our philosophies. We assume that homelessness has to do with economics, when it is more the mirror of the society and culture we have made.

Woodland *by Samuel Palmer.*

Care for our actual houses, then, however humble, is also care of the soul. No matter how little money we have, we can be mindful of the importance of beauty in our homes. No matter where we live, we live in a neighborhood, and we can cultivate this wider piece of earth, too, as our home, as a place that is integrally bound to the condition of our hearts.

Every home is a microcosm, the archetypal "world" embodied in a house or a plot of land or an apartment. Many traditions acknowledge the archetypal nature of a house with some kind of cosmic ornament—a sun and moon, a band of stars, a dome that obviously reflects the canopy of the sky. In its architecture and ornamentation, Shakespeare's Globe Theatre was the planet in miniature. Each of us lives in the Globe Theatre of our own homes; what happens to us there happens in our entire world.

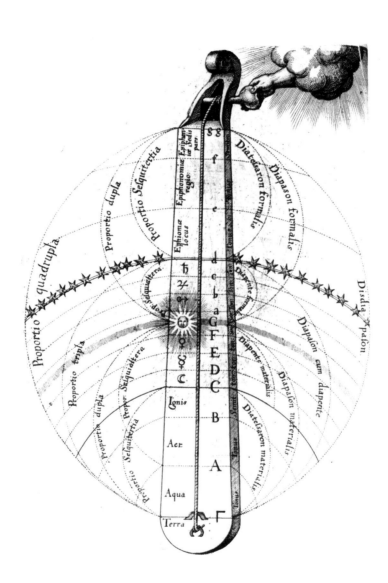

The Divine Harmony of the Universe *by Robert Fludd*.

The Psychopathology of Things

If things have soul, then they can also suffer and become neurotic: such is the nature of soul. Care of the soul therefore entails looking out for things, noticing where and how they are suffering, seeing their neuroses, and nursing them back to health. Robert Sardello suggests that a building have a resident therapist to take care of it in its suffering. He is not talking about care for the human residents, but for the building itself. His suggestion implies that we don't usually concern ourselves with the state of things, and tolerate much more ugliness and neglect in the things of our society than we should endure. We don't seem to realize how much our own pain reflects the diseases of our things.

In the idea of *anima mundi* there is no separation between our soul and the world soul. If the world is neurotic, we will share in that disorder. If we are depressed, it may be because we are living or working in a depressed building. Old illustrations, like the charts of the seventeenth-century magus Robert Fludd, show God tuning the great musical instrument of creation. On the strings of this great world guitar are angels, humans, and things. We all vibrate sympathetically like different octaves of the same tone, our human hearts pulsing in the same rhythms as those of the material and spiritual worlds. We participate in the fate and condition of our objects, just as they participate in ours.

The question Sardello asks, in the spirit of *anima mundi*, is a challenging one: Is the cancer that afflicts our human bodies essentially the same as the cancer we see corroding our cities? Is our personal health and the health of the world one and the same? We tend to think that the world is our enemy, that it is full of poisons that attack us, seeding us with illness and death. But if the world soul and our own souls are one, then as we neglect and abuse the things of the world, we are at the same time abusing ourselves.

Care of the soul requires that we have an eye and an ear for the world's suffering. In many American cities, streets and open spaces are littered with abandoned refuse—old tires, appliances, furniture, paper, garbage, rusty automobiles. Houses are boarded up, windows are smashed, wood is rotting, weeds have grown wild. We behold such a scene and think, the solution is to solve the problem of poverty. But why not feel for the things themselves. We are seeing things in a suffering condition—sick, broken, and dying. The disease before us is our failure in relation to the world. What is it in us that can allow the things of the world to become so distressed and to show so many symptoms without a nursing response from us? What are we doing when we treat things so badly?

When our citizens spray-paint a trolley or subway or a bridge or a sidewalk, clearly they are not just angry at society. They are raging at things. If we are going to understand our relationship with the things of the world, we have to find some insight into this anger, because at a certain level those people who are desecrating our public places are doing a job for us. We are implicated in their acting out.

Why does our culture seem so angry at things? Why do we take out our frustrations upon the very things that could potentially make our world into a satisfying and comforting home? One answer may be that when we are cut off from soul and its sensitivity to great spans of time and even timeless elements, we long painfully for an ideal future and for immortality. If our life efforts are directed toward making a new world, toward growth and constant improvement, then the past will be the enemy, a reminder of death.

Concentration on growth and change erodes appreciation for the eternal realities, those parts of the self that transcend the limits of ego. But soul loves the past and doesn't merely learn from history, it thrives on the stories and vestiges of what has been.

We are also angry at things that we feel no longer serve us. Many of the rusting objects that pollute our city streets are outmoded or no longer functioning tools. If we define a thing only in terms of its function, when it no longer functions we have no feeling for it. We discard it without a proper burial. And yet old things eventually reveal that they hold a great deal of soul. I live among many small old New England farms and frequently see, for example, an old horse-drawn rake sitting beautifully in a pasture, or an old barn leaning into the wind, or the shell of a once stately house transformed now into a splendid ruin. These bits of evidence of past times seem literally to glow with soul.

When things die to function, they can resurrect as images of history; and history is good food for the soul. We decorate our homes with antiques as a way of capturing soul, and museums are a focal point in our cities. In a world that denies death, vitality, too, may fade, for death and life are two sides of one coin. Or death may appear in literal form. Our trash, for instance, has become so haunting and demonic that we can no longer bury it. Its capacity to poison our world is becoming clearer, especially as we make things that have no death baked into them from the beginning. When we design things to be immortal, we are literalizing resurrection and immortality; when their usefulness has passed, things just won't go away. In an old movie starring Alec Guinness, *The Man in the White Suit*, a man invents a white suit that will never soil and never wear out. At first it seems like a triumph of technology and a gift to humankind. But soon it is revealed that this eternal suit is a curse, depriving workers of their livelihood and the process of manufacturing (which means, after all, working by hand) of its soul.

Ruins, like the old farm equipment in my neighbor's pastures, show us that something remains of beauty in a thing when its function has departed. Soul is then revealed, as though it had been hidden for years under well-oiled functioning. Soul is not about function, it is about beauty and form and memory. When the artist Merit Oppenheim got the crazy idea to line her teacup with fur, she was shocked to find her inspiration was thought to be a major artistic event. But she had found an elegant way to reveal the personality of the cup by eclipsing its function. Her revolutionary act was a breakthrough to soul, achieved by penetrating our dominant, blinding myth of use.

Beauty, the Face of the Soul

Throughout history we find certain schools of thought, such as the Renaissance Platonists and the Romantic poets, that have focused on the soul. It's interesting to note that these soul-minded writers have emphasized certain common themes. Relatedness, particularity, imagination, mortality, and pleasure are among them; another is beauty.

In a world where soul is neglected, beauty is placed last on its list of priorities. In the intellect-oriented curricula of our schools, for instance, science and math are considered important studies, because they allow further advances in technology. If there is a slash in funding, the arts are the first to go, even before athletics. The clear implication is that the arts are dispensable: we can't live without technology, but we can live without beauty.

This assumption that beauty is an accessory, and dispensable, shows that we don't understand the importance of giving the soul what it needs. The soul is nurtured by beauty. What food is to the

Primavera by Sandro Botticelli.

body, arresting, complex, and pleasing images are to the soul. I will go so far as to say that if we lack beauty in our lives, we will probably suffer familiar disturbances in the soul—depression, paranoia, meaninglessness, and addiction. The soul craves beauty and in its absence suffers what James Hillman has called "beauty neurosis."

Beauty assists the soul in its own peculiar ways of being. For example, beauty is arresting. For the soul, it is important to be taken out of the rush of practical life for the contemplation of timeless and eternal realities. Tradition named this need of the soul *vacatio*—a vacation from ordinary activity in favor of a moment of reflection and wonder. You may find yourself driving along a highway when you suddenly pass a vista that catches your breath. You stop the car, get out for just a few minutes, and behold the grandeur of nature. This is the arresting power of beauty, and giving in to that sudden longing of the soul is a way of giving it what it needs.

Some scholars say that the Three Graces dancing in a circle in Botticelli's famous painting *Primavera* represent Beauty, Restraint, and Pleasure. According to Renaissance writings, these three are the graces of life. What would a modern equivalent be—technology, information, and communication? The Renaissance graces have to do directly with the soul. Botticelli's painting shows Eros or Desire shooting his flaming arrow at Restraint. The arrow of desire and attachment stops us in our tracks—we are taken by the beauty, and feel its pleasure.

For the soul, then, beauty is not defined as pleasantness of form but rather as the quality in things that invites absorption and contemplation. Samiioetsu Yanagi, founder of Japan's modern craft movement, defines beauty as that which gives unlimited scope to the imagination; beauty is a source of imagination, he says, that never dries up. A thing so attractive and absorbing may not be pretty or pleasant. It could be ugly, in fact, and yet seize the soul as beautiful in this special sense. James Hillman defines beauty for the soul as things displaying themselves in their individuality. Yanagi's and Hillman's point is that beauty doesn't require prettiness. Some pieces of art are not pleasing to look at, and yet their content and form are arresting and lure the heart into profound imagination.

Le Bouquet Tout Fait *by Rene Magritte, 1957.*

Cornfield *by Samuel Palmer.*

An appreciation for beauty is simply an openness to the power of things to stir the soul. If we can be affected by beauty, then soul is alive and well in us, because the soul's great talent is for being affected. The word *passion* means basically "to be affected," and passion is the essential energy of the soul. The poet Rilke describes this passive power in the imagery of the flower's structure, when he calls it a "muscle of infinite reception." We don't often think of the capacity to be affected as strength and as the work of a powerful muscle, and yet for the soul, as for the flower, this is its toughest work and its main role in our lives.

Things Reanimated

At different times in our history we have denied soul to classes of beings we have wanted to control. Women, it was once said, have no soul. Slaves, the theological defense of a cruel system declared, have no soul. In our day we assume that things do not have soul, and thus we can do to them what we will. A revival of the doctrine of *anima mundi* would give soul back to the world of nature and artifact.

If we knew in our hearts that things have soul, we could not govern them as conscious subject over inert object. Instead, we would have a mutual relationship of affection, respect, and care. We would be less lonely in a world that is alive with its own kind of soul than we are in a mechanical world we think we need to sustain with our technological efforts.

Anima mundi is not a mystical philosophy requiring high forms of meditation, nor does it ask for a return to primitive animism. The sophisticated artists, theologians, and merchants of the Renaissance who lived this philosophy, such as Pico della Mirandola, Marsilio Ficino, and Lorenzo di Medici, are good examples for us. In their thought, their personal daily practices, and in the art and architecture they inspired, they cultivated a concrete world full of soul. The beauty of Renaissance art is inseparable from the soul-affirming philosophy that tutored it.

These Renaissance masters taught that we need to cultivate our relationship to the ensouled world through simple daily mindfulness and imaginative practices. They recommended careful exposure to specific kinds of music, art, food, landscapes, cultures, and climate. They were Epicureans of a sort, believing that things are rich in what they can offer the soul, but in order to receive that richness we must learn to enjoy things in moderation and use them with discrimination.

Neoplatonic philosophy taught these Renaissance masters of soul that soul straddles the eternal and the temporal, and that the full blend of these two dimensions gives life depth and vitality. Deep perspective in art reflected this profound perspective in thought. Ficino, a vegetarian, was sparse in his diet, and yet he was a connoisseur of fine wines. The Medicis could exercise their talent for commerce and banking and still recognize the importance of the arts and theology to the soul of their society. The secularism of our age, in contrast, forces religion and theology into a chamber, usually a university or a seminary, isolated from commerce and government. Yet soul requires a theological and artistic vision that influences every part of our lives.

Therefore, a revival of the worldview known as *anima mundi* is essential for a renewal of psychology and for genuine care of the soul. In the field of psychology, there have been attempts at alignment with religion, especially as we have tried to learn from Eastern religions the techniques and benefits of meditation and higher levels of consciousness. In theology and religion, it is common these days to find religious professionals training themselves in psychology and the social sciences. These two movements and others like them indicate a new awareness that religion, soul, and the world are profoundly implicated in each other. But we can't pursue that insight and also retain the prevailing worldview according to which the world is dead and subjectivity is limited to a reasoning ego. As so many commentators have pointed out, this bifurcated world is a characteristic of modern Western life that is not found in all cultures. We have created a comfortable and amazingly efficient life-style by means of this division, but we have won our pleasures and conveniences at the cost of soul.

There is no necessary enmity between technology and beauty, or between care of the soul and development of culture. Science has as much capacity for soulfulness as do art and religion. But in all these areas we have lived for a long time now as though soul were not a factor and consequently encounter soul only in intractable problems and deep-seated neuroses. For example, we have amazingly efficient cars, but marriage is becoming impossible to sustain. We produce movies and television programs without end, but we have little imagination about living in a peaceful international community. We have many instruments for medicine, but we don't understand except in the most rudimentary ways the relationship between life and disease. Once in our past, in Greek tragedies and comedies, a priest presided over the presentation of drama, indicating that going to the theater was a matter of life and death. Today we place theater and the other arts in the category of entertainment.

As long as we leave care of the soul out of our daily lives we will suffer the loneliness of living in a dead, cold, unrelated world. We can "improve" ourselves to the maximum, and yet we will still feel the alienation inherent in a divided existence. We will continue to exploit nature and our capacity to invent new things, but both will continue to overpower us, if we do not approach them with enough depth and imagination.

Frescoe, 1st c. BCE. Painted for the empress Livia, wife of emperor Augustus.

The way out of this neurosis is to leave our modern divisions behind and learn from other cultures, from art and religion, and from new movements in philosophy that there is another way to perceive the world. We can replace our modernist psychology with care of the soul, and we can begin building a culture that is sensitive to matters of the heart.

The Sacred Arts of Life

W E CAN RETURN NOW TO ONE OF PLATO'S EXPRESSIONS FOR CARE of the soul, *techne tou biou*, the craft of life. Care of the soul requires craft (*techne*)—skill, attention, and art. To live with a high degree of artfulness means to attend to the small things that keep the soul engaged in whatever we are doing, and it is the very heart of soul-making. From some grand overview of life, it may seem that only the big events are ultimately important. But to the soul, the most minute details and the most ordinary activities, carried out with mindfulness and art, have an effect far beyond their apparent insignificance.

Art is not found only in the painter's studio or in the halls of a museum, it also has its place in the store, the shop, the factory, and the home. In fact, when art is reserved as the province of professional artists, a dangerous gulf develops between the fine arts and the everyday arts. The fine arts are elevated and set apart from life, becoming too precious and therefore irrelevant. Having banished art to the museum, we fail to give it a place in ordinary life. One of the most effective forms of repression is to give a thing excessive honor.

The arts are important for all of us, whether or not we ourselves practice a particular discipline. Art, broadly speaking, is that which invites us into contemplation—a rare commodity in modern life. In that moment of contemplation, art intensifies the presence of the world. We see it more vividly and more deeply. The emptiness that many people complain dominates their lives comes in part from a failure to let the world in, to perceive it and engage it fully. Naturally, we'll feel empty if everything we do slides past without sticking.

Autumn Grasses and Silver Moon, *Screen, 18th c., Japan.*

Window *by Pierre Bonnard.*

Living artfully, therefore, might require something as simple as *pausing*. Some people are incapable of being arrested by things because they are always on the move. A common symptom of modern life is that there is no time for thought, or even for letting impressions of a day sink in. Yet it is only when the world enters the heart that it can be made into soul. The vessel in which soul-making takes place is an inner container scooped out by reflection and wonder. There is no doubt that some people could spare themselves the expense and trouble of psychotherapy simply by giving themselves a few minutes each day for quiet reflection. This simple act would provide what is missing in their lives: a period of non-doing that is essential nourishment to the soul.

Akin to pausing, and just as important in care of the soul, is *taking time*. I realize these are extremely simple suggestions, but taken to heart they could transform a life, by allowing soul to enter. Taking time with things, we get to know them more intimately and to feel more genuinely connected to them.

Living artfully might require taking the time to buy things with soul for the home. Good linens, a special rug, or a simple teapot can be a source of enrichment not only in our own life, but also in the lives of our children and grandchildren. The soul basks in this extended sense of time. But we can't discover the soul in a thing without first taking time to observe it and be with it for a while. This kind of observation has a quality of intimacy about it; it's not just studying a consumer guide for factual and technical analysis.

The ordinary arts we practice every day at home are of more importance to the soul than their simplicity might suggest. For example, I can't explain it, but I enjoy doing dishes. I've had an automatic dishwasher in my home for over a year, and I have never used it. What appeals to me, as I think about it, is the reverie induced by going through the ritual of washing, rinsing, and drying.

I also cherish the opportunity to hang clothes on a line outdoors. The fresh smell, the wet fabrics, the blowing wind, and the drying sun go together to make an experience of nature and culture that is unique and particularly pleasurable for its simplicity.

Jean Lall, the astrologer, observes that daily life at home is full of epiphanies. "Within our daily experience," she writes, "as keepers of home and gardens the spirits still move and speak if we but attend. They slip in through the cracks, making themselves felt in little breakdowns in appliances, unplanned sproutings in the flowerbeds, and sudden moments of blinding beauty, as where sunlight glances across a newly-waxed table or the wind stirs clean laundry into fresh choreography."

Many of the arts practiced at home are especially nourishing to the soul because they foster contemplation and demand a degree of artfulness, such as arranging flowers, cooking, and making repairs. I have a friend who is taking time over several months to paint a garden scene on a low panel of her dining room wall. Sometimes these ordinary arts bring out the individual, so that when you go into a home you can see the special character of your hosts in a particular aspect of their home.

When imagination is allowed to move to deep places, the sacred is revealed. The more different kinds of thoughts we experience around a thing and the deeper our reflections go as we are arrested by its artfulness, the more fully its sacredness can emerge. It follows, then, that living artfully can be a tonic for the secularization of life that characterizes our time. We can, of course, bring religion more closely in tune with ordinary life by immersing ourselves in formal rituals and traditional teachings; but we can also serve religion's soul by discovering the "natural religion" in all things. The route to this discovery is art, both the fine arts and those of everyday life. If we could loosen our grip on the functionality of life and let ourselves be arrested by the imaginal richness that surrounds all objects, natural and human-made, we might ground our secular attitudes in a religious sensibility and give ordinary life soul.

The medieval idea about learning, that theology is the ultimate science and all the others are "ancillary"—in humble service—is, to me, absolutely correct. Every issue, no matter how secular it appears to be, has a sacred dimension. If you press anything far enough, you will come up against either the holy or the demonic. Our secular sciences of physics, sociology, psychology, and the rest stop short of theo-

Woman in the Forest *by Joan Hanley.*

logical categories, thus preserving their scientific "objectivity," but also losing soul. Religious sensibility and soul are inseparable. I'm not saying that any particular religious affiliation or belief is essential to soul, but that a solid, palpable, and intellectually satisfying appreciation of the sacred is a sine qua non of living soulfully. Recall Nicholas of Cusa's observation that God is the minimum as well as the maximum. The small things in everyday life are no less sacred than the great issues of human existence. It is a daily involvement in mysteries and a personal quest for a corresponding ethic. Without soul, religion's truths and moral principles might be believed in, perhaps, and discussed, but they are not taken truly to heart and lived from the core of one's being.

Dreams: A Royal Road to Soul

Care of the soul involves "work," in the alchemical sense. It is impossible to care for the soul and live at the same time in unconsciousness. Sometimes soul work is exciting and inspiring, but often it is also challenging, requiring genuine courage. Rarely easy, work with the soul is usually placed squarely in that place we would rather not visit, in that emotion we don't want to feel, and in that understanding we would prefer to do without. The most honest route may be the most difficult to take. It is not easy to visit the place in ourselves that is most challenging and to look straight into the image that gives us the most fright; yet, there, where the work is most intense, is the source of soul.

Since we never want to take up the piece of our emotion that is most in need of attention, I usually recommend to my patients that they give increased awareness to their dreams; for there they will find images that in waking life are very difficult to face. Dreams truly are the mythology of the soul and working with them forms a major piece in the project of making life more artful.

Therapeutic work with dreams could be a model for less formal habits of giving dreams a serious place in our ordinary lives. When a person comes to me for an hour of therapy, I like to hear a dream or two early in the session. I don't like to listen to a dream and then immediately reach for an interpretation. It is better to let the dream lead us into new territory than to try to master the dream and figure it out at once. After the dream has been told, we might go on to talk about the person's life, since the therapy is almost always concerned with life situations. I may notice ways in which the dream offers us images and a language for talking about life with depth and imagination. Instead of trying to figure out the dream, we are letting the dream figure us out, allowing the dream to influence and shape our way of imagining.

In therapy it's tempting for both therapist and patient to translate a dream into theories and rationalizations that merely support the ideas of the therapist or the problematical attitudes of the patient. It is much better to let the dream interpret us rather than for us to become clever in interpreting the dream in ways most compatible with our existing ideas.

It is my experience that a dream reveals itself to the patient and the therapist slowly, gradually. Having patience with dreams is extremely important, and is more effective in the long run than any exercise of knowledge, techniques, and tricks. The dream reveals itself on its own timetable, but it does reveal itself.

It's important to trust your intuitions, which are not the same as your intellectual interpretations. For example, sometimes a person will tell me a dream and immediately recommend a way of understanding it or offer a bias toward one of the characters. A woman, for instance, relates a dream in which she has absent-mindedly left her front door open, allowing a man to sneak into her house. "It was a nightmare," she says. "I think the dream is telling me that I'm not careful enough about keeping myself protected. I'm too open."

You see, I'm given a dream and an interpretation. Even though I have considerable experience working with dreams and have been trained not to buy into whatever idea a patient gives me, I'm sometimes unconsciously affected by the interpretation. It's so reasonable. Of course, she is too vulnerable and is threatened by an intruder. But then I remember my first rule: trust your intuitions. I wonder if the "accidental" opening in the door might not be a good thing for this person. The opening may allow new personalities to enter her living space.

There is often an apparent collusion between the dream-ego and the waking dreamer. As the dreamer tells the dream, she may slant her story in the direction of the "I" in the dream, thus convincing the listener to take a certain position in relation to the figures in the dream. Therefore, perhaps sometimes too much in compensation, I like to assume a rather perverse attitude when I hear the dream. I make a point of considering an angle different from the dreamer's. To put it more technically, I assume that in the telling of the dream the dreamer may be locked in the same complex as is the dream-ego. If I simply accept what the dreamer tells me, I may get caught in the dreamer's complex, and then I'm of no use. So I say to this dreamer: "Maybe it's not so bad that your usual thought about closing doors failed in this case. Maybe it allowed an entry that will prove to be beneficial. At least we can keep an open mind."

A woman who is a writer tells a dream in which she catches a friend of hers smearing crayons all over the dreamer's typewriter. "It was an awful dream," she said, "and I know what it means. My inner child is always interfering with my adult work. If only I could grow up!"

Notice that this person, too, is quick to move toward interpretation. More than that, she wants me to take a certain position in relation to her dream.

"Was your friend in the dream a child?" I ask.

"No, she was an adult. She was the age she is in life."

"Then why do you think she is being childish?"

"Crayons are a childish thing," she says as if stating the obvious.

"Can you tell me something about this friend of yours?" I am trying to break free of her strong views about her dream.

"She's very seductive, always wearing outlandish clothes—you know, bright colors and always low-cut."

"Is it possible," I say, taking a leap on the basis of her association, "that this colorful, sensual woman could be adding color, body, and some positive qualities of the child to your writing?"

Sleeping Gypsy *by Henri Rousseau.*

The Dreamer (Der Traum) *by Max Klinger.*

"I suppose it's possible," she says, still unconvinced by this affront to her more satisfying interpretation.

One of the things that turned me away from her reading of the dream, apart from the general principle that we should avoid getting caught in the dream ego's complexes, was the negative narcissism in her judgment about the child: she didn't want to accept her own childlike ways. Once we moved away from her attachment to her usual way of thinking about herself, an attitude that strongly colored her own thoughts about the dream, we could go on to consider some truly fresh ideas about her life situation and her personal habits.

Another rule of thumb about dreams is that there is never a single, definitive reading. A dream may survive a lifetime of neglect or an onslaught of interpretations and remain an icon and a fertile enigma for years of reflection. The point in working with a dream is never to translate it into a final meaning, but always to give it honor and respect, drawing from it as much meaningfulness and imaginative meditation as possible. Entering a dream should revitalize the imagination, not keep it in fixed and tired habits.

The desire to squeeze a single meaning out of a dream or a work of art or a tale from life is inherently and profoundly Promethean. We want to steal fire from the gods for the sake of humanity. We want to replace divine mystery with human rationality. But this loss of complexity and mystery in our everyday response to life stories entails a loss of soul as well, because soul always manifests itself in mystery and multiplicity.

Dreams themselves often show us the way to understand them: they pull the dreamer deep into a body of water, or down into a pit, or down an elevator to a basement, or down a dark stairway, or deep into an alley. Typically, the dreamer, preferring height and light, is afraid to make the downward move into darkness. When I taught in the university, students frequently told me dreams of going into the library, getting on an elevator, then finding themselves in an ancient basement. The dream is not surprising, given the fact that the life of academia is so much an Apollonic, upper-world, ivory tower affair, and stands as a metaphor for all our attempts at understanding.

The Guiding Daimon

An approach often taken to images is to find a meaning outside the image itself. A cigar in a dream is considered a phallic symbol instead of a cigar. A woman is an anima figure instead of a particular woman. A child is the "child part of myself" instead of simply the child of the dream. We think of imagination as a kind of symbolic thinking, with, as Freud put it, a latent and a manifest meaning. If we could "decipher" the given symbols, to use a popular rationalistic word, we could learn the meaning that is hidden in the image.

But there is another possible way to understand the creations of the dream world. What if there were no hidden meaning, no underlying message? What if we chose to confront images in all their mystery, deciding whether to follow their lead or to struggle with them?

The Greeks referred to the multitude of unnamed spirits that motivate and guide life as daimons. Socrates claimed to have lived his life according to the dictates of his daimon. In more recent times, W. B. Yeats warned that the daimon both inspires and threatens. In the chapter of *Memories, Dreams, Reflections* entitled "Late Thoughts," Jung, too, discusses the daimon. "We know that something unknown, alien, does come our way, just as we know that we do not ourselves *make* a dream or an inspiration, but that it somehow arises of its own accord. What does happen to us in this manner can be said to emanate from mana, from a daimon, a god, or the unconscious." He goes on to say that he prefers the term *the unconscious*, but he might just as well say *daimon*. Daimonic living is a response to the movements of imagination. When Jung was building his tower, workmen delivered a large piece of stone that was the wrong size. He took this "mistake" as the work of his Mercurial daimon and used the stone for one of his most important sculptures, the Bollingen Stone.

One implication of offering respect to the dream world is that we have to re-imagine imagination itself. Instead of seeing it as a particularly creative form of mind work, we could understand it more along Greek mythological lines, as a spring from which autonomous beings arise. We would realize that the images of dreams and art are not puzzles to be solved, and that imagination hides its meaningfulness as much as it reveals it. In order to be affected by a dream, it isn't necessary to understand it or even to mine it for meanings. Merely giving our attention to such imagery, granting its autonomy and mystery, goes a long way toward shifting the center of consciousness from understanding to response. To live in the presence of the daimonic is to obey inner laws and urgencies.

The source from which life flows is so deep that it is experienced as "other." Speaking in the ancient language of the daimonic helps bring imagination into our very sense of self. Our relationship to the deep source of life becomes interpersonal, a dramatic tension between self and angel. In this dialogue, life also becomes more artful, in some cases even dramatic. We see this in people we label psychotic. Most of their actions are explicitly dramatic. Their deep "others," the personalities who play significant roles in their lives, appear in full dress. Writers talk about the characters of their fiction as people with will and intention. The novelist Margaret Atwood said

Closet *by Thomas McAnulty.*

once in an interview, "If the author gets too bossy, the characters may remind her that, though she is their creator, they are to some extent her creator as well."

Art teaches us to respect imagination as something far beyond human creation and intention. To live our ordinary life artfully is to have this sensibility about the things of daily life, to live more intuitively and to be willing to surrender a measure of our rationality and control in return for the gifts of soul.

The Soul Arts

Care of the soul may take the form of living in a fully embodied imagination, being an artist at home and at work. You don't have to be a professional in order to bring art into the care of your soul; anyone can have an art studio at home, for instance. Like Jung, Black Elk, and Ficino, we could decorate our homes with images from our dreams and waking fantasy.

One of my own forms of expression is to play the piano in times of strong emotion. I remember well the day Martin Luther King, Jr., was killed. I was so overwhelmed that I went to the piano and played Bach for three hours. The music gave form and voice to my scrambled emotions, without explanations and rational interpretations.

The stuff of the world is there to be made into images that become for us tabernacles of spirituality and containers of mystery. If we don't allow soul its place in our lives, we are forced to encounter these mysteries in fetishes and symptoms, which in a sense are pathological art forms, the gods in our diseases. The example of artists teaches us that every day we can transform ordinary experience into the material of soul—in diaries, poems, drawings, music, letters, watercolors.

As we read our experiences and learn to express them artfully, we are making life more soulful. Our homely arts arrest the flow of life momentarily so that events can be submitted to the alchemy of reflection. In a letter to a friend, we can deepen the impressions of experience and settle them in the heart, where they can become the foundation for soul. Our great museums of art are simply a grand model for the more modest museum that is our home. There is no reason not to imagine our own homes as a place where the Muses can do their work of inspiration daily.

Children paint every day and love to show their works on walls and refrigerator doors. But as we become adults, we abandon this important soul task of childhood. We assume, I suppose, that children are just learning motor coordination and alphabets. But maybe they are doing something more fundamental: finding forms that reflect what is going on in their souls. When we grow up and begin to think of the art gallery as much more advanced than the refrigerator door, we lose an important ritual of childhood, giving it away to the professional artist. We are then left with mere rational reasons for our lives, feelings of emptiness and confusion, expensive visits to a psychotherapist, and a compulsive attachment to pseudoimages, such as shallow television programs. When our own images no longer have a home, a personal museum, we drown our sense of loss in pale substitutes, trashy novels or formulaic movies.

As the poets and painters of centuries have tried to tell us, art is not about the expression of talent or the making of pretty things. It is about the preservation and containment of soul. It is about arresting life and making it available for contemplation. Art captures the eternal in the everyday, and it is the eternal that feeds soul—the whole world in a grain of sand.

Leonardo da Vinci asks an interesting question in one of his notebooks: "Why does the eye see a thing more clearly in dreams than the imagination when awake?" One answer is that the eye of the soul perceives the eternal realities so important to the heart. In waking life, most of us see only with our physical eyes, even though we could, with some effort of imagination, glimpse fragments of eternity in the most ordinary passing events. Dream teaches us to look with that other eye, the eye that in waking life belongs to the artist, to each of us as artist.

A soul-centered understanding of art sees the interpenetration of poetic image and ordinary life. Art shows us what is already there in the ordinary, but without art we live under the illusion that there is only time, and not eternity. As we practice our daily arts, if only in the composing of a heartfelt letter, we are unearthing the eternal from within ordinary time, engaging in the special qualities, themes, and circumstances of the soul. Soul thrives as we jot down a thought in our diary or note a dream, and give body to a slight influx of eternity. Our notebooks then truly become our own private gospels and sutras, our holy books, and our simple paintings truly serve as icons, every bit as significant in the work of our own soul as the wonderful icons of the Eastern churches are for their congregations.

Care of the soul is not a project of self-improvement nor a way of being released from the troubles and pains of human existence. It is not at all concerned with living properly or with emotional health. These are the concerns of temporal, heroic, Promethean life. Care of the soul touches another dimension, in no way separate from life, but not identical either with the problem solving that occupies so much of our consciousness. We care for the soul solely by honoring its expressions, by giving it time and opportunity to reveal itself, and by living life in a way that fosters the depth, interiority, and quality in which it flourishes. Soul is its own purpose and end.

To the soul, memory is more important than planning, art more compelling than reason, and love more fulfilling than understanding. We know we are well on the way toward soul when we feel attachment to the world and the people around us and when we live as much from the heart as from the head. We know soul is being cared for when our pleasures feel deeper than usual, when we can let go of the need to be free of complexity and confusion, and when compassion takes the place of distrust and fear. Soul is interested in the differences among cultures and individuals, and within ourselves it wants to be expressed in uniqueness if not in outright eccentricity.

Therefore, when in the midst of my confusion and my stumbling attempts to live a transparent life, *I* am the fool, and not everyone around me, then I know I am discovering the power of the soul to make a life interesting. Ultimately, care of the soul results in an individual "I" I never would have planned for or maybe even wanted. By caring for the soul faithfully, every day, we step out of the way and let our full genius emerge. Soul coalesces into the mysterious philosophers' stone, that rich, solid core of personality the alchemists sought, or it opens into the peacock's tail—a revelation of the soul's colors and a display of its dappled brilliance.

Study of Weeds *by Albrecht Durer, 1471–1528.*

SUGGESTIONS FOR FURTHER READING

Ficino, Marsilio. *Marsilio Ficino: The Book of Life.* Translated by Charles Boer. Dallas: Spring Publications, 1980.

An excellent translation of a fifteenth-century book. Because of its antique style, it is not easy to follow, but taken a little at a time, and thought of metaphorically, it offers many good suggestions for care of the soul.

Hillman, James. *A Blue Fire: Selected Writings by James Hillman.* Edited by Thomas Moore. New York: Harper & Row, 1989.

This anthology of James Hillman's writings provides an overview of his thinking. An introduction to the book summarizes Hillman's "archetypal psychology," and brief introductions to each chapter guide the reader through his ideas. Hillman is the foremost spokesperson today for a soul-oriented psychology.

The Homeric Hymns. Translated by Charles Boer. 5th ed. Dallas: Spring Publications, 1991.

A readable, poetic, beautiful translation of hymns that tell the stories and offer praise to Hera, Aphrodite, Hermes, Demeter, and many other gods and goddesses of the Greeks.

Jung, C. G. *Memories, Dreams, Reflections.* Edited by Aniela Jaffé and translated by Richard and Clara Winston. New York: Pantheon Books, 1973.

I think it is best to approach Jung for the first time through his memoirs and "late thoughts." This is a unique "autobiography," telling the story of a soul rather than a life.

Kerényi, Karl. *The Gods of the Greeks.* Translated by Norman Cameron. London: Thames and Hudson, 1974.

This book has long been my choice as a source for Greek mythological stories and characters. Well-documented, it remains close to classical sources and yet conveys the stories with charm and wit.

Rilke, Rainer Maria. *Letters to a Young Poet.* Translated by Stephen Mitchell. New York: Random House, 1984.

Rilke is an important source for care of the soul because his own perceptions are extraordinarily profound and subtle, and they are presented in his prose and poetry with all the paradox in language and meaning they deserve.

Sardello, Robert. *Facing the World with Soul*. Hudson, N.Y.: Lindisfarne Press, 1991.

This book contains Sardello's fascinating work on soul in the world, as well as his unique approach to spirituality. He constantly surprises with the freshness of his approach to such common themes as economics, things, architecture, medicine, and herpes.

Sexson, Lynda. *Ordinarily Sacred*. New York: Crossroad, 1982.

Lynda Sexson offers a theology of everyday experience in this enchanting book that shows how the religious traditions of the world lie slightly concealed in the details and commonplaces of ordinary life.

Wilde, Oscar. *De Profundis and Other Writings*. New York: Penguin Books, 1973.

Wilde's notorious light wit turned dark in this long reflection affected by his experience of prison. For me, its importance lies in its Romantic reading of Christianity. Wilde may sound heretical, but it is always good to read heresies for the counterpoint they give orthodoxy, allowing us to hear the full music in any religion or philosophy.

Yanagi, Soetsu. *The Unknown Craftsman: A Japanese Insight into Beauty*. Adapted by Bernard Leach. Rev. ed. New York: Kodansha International, 1989.

This book is full of insights into the nature of art, beauty, and craft. Like the other books I am recommending, it is not a straightforward simplification of these difficult subjects. It is not even fully coherent, yet it keeps the grounding soul in an area that too easily floats off into abstractions and idealizations.

ACKNOWLEDGMENTS

FRONT COVER: *Woman Sewing Before a Garden Window* by Edouard Vuillard, Museum of Fine Arts, Boston

PAGE 11: *John Keats* by Joseph Severn, © National Portrait Gallery, London

PAGE 13: *Mystery* by Odilon Redon, © Art Resource, New York

PAGE 17: Bronze sculpture of Lao Tzu riding a bull, © Bridgeman Art Library, London

PAGE 18: Portrait of Sigmund Freud, © Bridgeman Art Library, London

PAGE 19: Sigmund Freud boarding a plane, © Art Resource, New York

PAGE 21: *Puberty* by Edvard Munch, © Art Resource, New York

PAGES 22 AND 23: *Creation* and *Wheel of Life* by Hildegard of Bingen, © Art Resource, New York

PAGE 24: *La Minotauromachie* by Pablo Picasso, © Art Resource, New York

PAGE 25: Portrait of Emily Dickenson, © Art Resource, New York

PAGE 26: *Victorian Family Group*, © MoonRunner Design, Dorset, England

PAGE 27: *Family in a Horse-Drawn Carriage* by Rousseau, © Art Resource, New York

PAGES 28–29: *The Wedding* by Henri Rousseau, © Musee de l'Orangerie, Paris, France

PAGE 31: Top, *Odysseus and the Sirens*, © British Museum, London

PAGE 32: *Painter of Orythia* Red figure crater from Campania, © Museo Archeologico, Palermo, Italy

PAGE 38: *Persephone*, © Art Resource, New York

PAGE 39: *Funerary amphora with Ulysses, Agamemnon and Diomedes,* © Museo Archeologico, Florence, Italy

PAGE 40: *Rape of Europa* © Museo di Villa Giulia, Rome, Italy

PAGE 41: *Hades and Persephone* © Erich Lessing, Munich, Germany

PAGE 42: *Mary and Child*, © Sotheby's Art, London

PAGE 45: *Enigma dell'ora* by Giorgio de Chirico, © VAGA, New York, NY

PAGES 46–47: *Narcissus and Echo* by Nicholas Poussin, © Art Resource, New York

PAGES 52–53: *Narcissus and Echo* by John William Waterhouse, © Art Resource, New York

PAGE 57: *Wanderer Overlooking a Sea of Fog* by Caspar David Friedrich, © Kunsthalle, Hamburg

PAGE 58: *Les Yeaux Clos* by Odilon Redon, © Sotheby's Art, London

PAGE 61: *Narcissus* by Gustave Moreau, © Musée Gustave Moreau

PAGE 65: *Il Bacio* by Francesco Hayez © Pinacoteca di Brera, Milan, Italy

PAGE 67: Sigmund Freud, © Bridgeman Art Library, London

PAGE 68: *Eros and Psyche,* © Art Resource, New York

PAGE 69: *Tristan and Isolde,* © Art Resource, New York

PAGE 71: *Tristan and Isolde,* © Bridgeman Art Library, London

PAGE 75: *Queen in Her Tower,* © Metropolitan Museum of Modern Art, New York

PAGE 76: *The Birthday* by Marc Chagall, © Metropolitan Museum of Modern Art, New York

PAGE 79: *Bego with Company* by Niko Pirosmanashvili, © Bridgeman Art Library, London

PAGE 81: *The Evocation of the Butterflies,* © Institute of the Arts, Detroit

PAGES 82–83: *Jealousy* by Edvard Munch, © Art Resource, New York

PAGE 84: *Il Parnasso* by Andrea Mantegna, © Art Resource, New York

PAGES 92–93: *The Dance of Life* by Edvard Munch, © Art Resource, New York

PAGE 94: *Sidonia von Bork* by Edward Burne-Jones, © Tate Gallery, London

PAGES 96–97: *East Twefth Street* by Ben Shahn, © Estate of Ben Shahn—Licensed by VAGA, New York, NY

PAGE 100: Korum kapi prayer rug in silk and metal-thread, © Christie's Art, Oxford

PAGE 103: *Trouble* by Ben Shahn, © Estate of Ben Shahn—Licensed by VAGA, New York, NY

PAGES 104–105: *The Body of Abel Found by Adam and Eve* by William Blake, © Tate Gallery, London

PAGE 106: *Discord* by Ben Shahn, © Estate of Ben Shahn—Licensed by VAGA, New York, NY

PAGE 109: Portrait of Oscar Wilde, © Art Resource, New York

PAGE 110: *Christ Between the Two Thieves* by Rembrandt van Rijn, © Art Resource, New York

PAGE 113: *Melancholia* by Albrecht Durer, © Art Resource, New York

PAGE 117: Self portrait by William Kane, © Carnegie Institute Museum of Art, Pittsburgh

PAGES 120–121: *The Racetrack* by Albert Pinkham Ryder, © Cleveland Museum of Art

PAGE 124: *Figure in a Landscape,* © Premgit, Dorset, England

PAGE 126: *Daphne* by Joan Hanley, © Joan Hanley

PAGE 131: Relationship between the organs of the body, the humors and the Zodiac, © Art Resource, New York

PAGE 133: The Mask by Navyo, © MoonRunner Design

PAGE 134: *Storm in Tropical Forest with Tigers—Surprise!* by Henri Rousseau, © Art Resource, New York

PAGE 136: *Tiger,* Sotheby's National History Atlas, © Sotheby's Art, London

PAGE 139: *Melothisia,* © Art Resource, New York

PAGE 140: *Aeschylus,* © Bridgeman Art Library, London

PAGE 143: *Temple of Music* by Robert Fludd, © Art Resource, New York

PAGE 144: *The Tree,* a lithograph by Odilon Redon, © Christie's Art, Oxford

PAGE 146: Portrait of Ralph Waldo Emerson, © Art Resource, New York

PAGES 148–149: *Nighthawks* by Edward Hopper, © Art Resource, New York

PAGE 151: *Dining Room* in the Country by Pierre Bonnard, © Art Resource, New York

PAGE 154: *The Lacemaker* by Johannes Vermeer van Delft, © Art Resource, New York

PAGE 157: *The Alchemist,* © Art Resource, New York

PAGE 158: *Interior* by Gwen John, © Art Resource, New York

PAGE 161: *The Money Lenders* by Quentin Massys, © Louvre Museum, Paris

PAGE 167: *Inside Looking Out* by Ben Shahn, © Estate of Ben Shahn—Licensed by VAGA, New York, NY

PAGES 170–171: *The River of Life* by William Blake, © Art Resource, New York

PAGES 174–175: *Christina's World* by Andrew Wyeth, © Art Resource, New York

PAGE 178: *A Hilly Scene* by Samuel Palmer, © Art Resource, New York

PAGE 181: *The Angelus* by Jean-Francois Millet, © Musee d'Orsay, Paris

PAGE 184: *Aztec Eagle Warrior,* © Michael Zabe

PAGE 188: *St. Bernard Preaching to Cistercian Monks,* © Giraudon, Paris

PAGE 192: Marsilio Ficino, a sculpture by Andrea Ferucci, © Bridgeman Art Library, London

PAGE 196: Portrait of Thomas Moore, © Art Resource, New York

PAGE 198: *Baptism of Christ* by Piero della Francesca, © Art Resource, New York

PAGE 201: *Remaining in the Middle* by Navyo, © MoonRunner Design, Dorset, England

PAGE 202: *Icarus and Daedalus,* © Art Resource, New York

PAGES 204–205: *The Fall of Icarus* by Pieter Breughel the Elder, © Art Resource, New York

PAGE 206: *Actaeon torn by his dogs,* © Art Resource, New York

PAGE 209: *Pegasus Departing* by Alfred Pinkham Ryder, © National Museum of American Art, The Smithsonian, Washington

PAGE 216: *Wisconsin Farm Scene* by Paul A. Seifert, © New York State History Association

PAGE 219: *Woodland* by Samuel Palmer, © Tate Gallery, London

PAGE 220: *The Divine Harmony of the Universe* by Robert Fludd, © Art Resource, New York

PAGE 223: *Cup and Saucer,* © Metropolitan Museum of Modern Art, New York

PAGES 224–225: *La Primavera* by Sandro Botticelli, © Art Resource, New York

PAGE 227: *Le Bouquet Tout Fait* by René Magritte, © Christie's Art, Oxford

PAGE 228: *Cornfield* by Samuel Palmer, © Tate Gallery, London

PAGE 233: *Autumn Grasses and Silver Moon,* © Sotheby's Art, London

PAGE 234: *Window* by Pierre Bonnard, © Art Resource, New York

PAGE 237: *Woman in the Forest* by Joan Hanley, © Joan Hanley

PAGES 240–241: *Sleeping Gypsy* by Henri Rousseau, © Metropolitan Museum of Modern Art, New York

PAGE 242: *The Dreamer (Der Traum)* by Max Klinger, © Staatliche Graphische Sammlung, Munich

PAGE 245: *Closet* by Thomas McAnulty, © Thomas McAnulty

PAGE 249: *Study of Weeds* by Albrecht Durer, © Bridgeman Art Library, London